T0338518

INTEGRATED NATURAL LANGUAGE DIALOGUE

THE KLUWER INTERNATIONAL SERIES
IN ENGINEERING AND COMPUTER SCIENCE

NATURAL LANGUAGE PROCESSING
AND MACHINE TRANSLATION

Consulting Editor

Jaime Carbonell

INTEGRATED NATURAL LANGUAGE DIALOGUE

A COMPUTATIONAL MODEL

Robert E. Frederking

Siemens, A.G.

KLUWER ACADEMIC PUBLISHERS
Boston/Dordrecht/Lancaster

Distributors for North America:
Kluwer Academic Publishers
101 Philip Drive
Assinippi Park
Norwell, Massachusetts 02061 USA

Distributors for the UK and Ireland:
Kluwer Academic Publishers
MTP Press Limited
Falcon House, Queen Square
Lancaster LAI IRN, UNITED KINGDOM

Distributors for all other countries:
Kluwer Academic Publishers Group
Distribution Centre
Post Office Box 322
3300 AH Dordrecht, THE NETHERLANDS

Library of Congress Cataloging-in-Publication Data

Frederking, Robert E.
  Integrated natural language dialoque / by Robert E. Frederking.
     p. cm. — (The Kluwer international series in engineering and
computer science ; SECS 41. Natural language processing and machine
translation)
  Bibliography: p.
  Includes index.
  ISBN 0-89838-255-6 : $45.00 (est.)
  1. Psli3 (Computer system) 2. Linguistics—Data processing.
I. Title. II. Series: Kluwer international series in engineering
and computer science ; SECS 41. III. Series: Kluwer international
series in engineering and computer science. Natural language
processing and machine translation.
P98.F68 1988   87-26857
410 '.28 '5—dc19   CIP

Printed in the United States of America

To Barb and Blanche

Table of Contents

List of Figures

List of Tables

Preface

Natural language dialogue is a continuous, unified phenomenon. Speakers use their conversational context to simplify individual utterances through a number of linguistic devices, including ellipsis and definite references. Yet most computational systems for using natural language treat individual utterances as separate entities, and have distinctly separate processes for handling ellipsis, definite references, and other dialogue phenomena.

This book, a slightly revised version of the Ph.D. dissertation that I completed in December 1986, describes a different approach. It presents a computational system, Psli3, that uses the uniform framework of a production system architecture to carry out natural language understanding and generation in a well-integrated way. This is demonstrated primarily through intersentential ellipsis resolution, in addition to examples of definite reference resolution and interactive error correction. The system's conversational context arises naturally as the result of the persistence of the internal representations of previous utterances in working memory. Natural language input is interpreted within this framework using a modification of the syntactic technique of chart parsing, extended to include semantics, and adapted to the production system architecture. This technique, called semantic chart parsing, provides a graceful way of handling ambiguity within this architecture, and allows separate knowledge sources to interact smoothly across different utterances in a highly integrated fashion.

The design of this system demonstrates how flexible and natural user interactions can be carried out using a system with a naturally flexible control structure. In addition, a processing-based taxonomy for ellipsis resolution that we developed is used to analyze our coverage of intersentential ellipsis. The semantic chart parser is further extended to allow several closely related sentences to be treated in a single chart. This allows the relationship between the sentences to be used in a simple way to select between competing alternate interpretations, and provides a natural means of resolving complex elliptical utterances.

The resulting system is described in detail, and extensive examples of the system's processing of user interactions are presented. The major advantage of this book over the dissertation is the presence of an index, which frees the reader from having to memorize the whole work in order to find something again later.

It is now my pleasure to thank those who helped make this work easier, or even possible:

- my advisor, Jaime G. Carbonell, a continuous source of inspiration and detailed comments, despite his impressive number of commitments. I will be pleased if I approach the level of any one of his many achievements.

- my thesis committee: Phil Hayes, Rich Thomason, and Herb Simon. This work has been distinctly improved in response to their comments.

- other technical influences: John Anderson, Allen Newell, Dana Scott, David Evans, Jon Doyle, Lori Levin, and others who commented on my thesis proposal, or influenced my approach to production systems and artificial intelligence.

- Steve Clark, Doug Reece, and a number of people at Siemens AG, especially my coworkers at the Corporate Laboratories for Information Technology in Munich, for help and support in producing this book from the dissertation. Siemens also helped motivate me to finally finish my degree, with an overseas job offer.

- Rene Nuijens, a Dutch graphic artist working in Munich, for the cover drawing, which is a stylized representation of a banyan tree, a tropical tree with many trunks.

- friends at Carnegie Group Inc: Peggy Andersen, Scott Safier, Monica Cellio, Sean Winters, Peter Neuss, and Thelma McGough. Artificial intelligence for fun and profit. Who would have thought it possible?

- friends in the XCALIBUR project: Steve Morrisson, Marion Kee, Mark Boggs, Ira Monarch, Michael "Fuzzy" Mauldin and Ben MacLaren. My first involvement with ellipsis in natural language.

- the folks in the Intelligent Systems Lab of the Robotics Institute when I was there: Mark Fox, Donald Kosy, Brad Allen, Mark Wright, Gary Strohm, and Joe Mattis. Psli3 was born there.

- my wife Barb and our rabbit Blanche, for affection and intellectual stimulation.

- my family, for constant emotional support; Bill Marx, Gregg Podnar, Nelson Oliver, and other friends; and the CMU CSD community, still the best place in the world to do computer science research.

And last but not least:

This research was supported by the Digital Equipment Corporation XSEL project, the National Library of Medicine under contract N01-LM-4-3529, and the Office of Naval Research under contract N00014-82-C-0767. This research was also supported by a fellowship from the National Science Foundation under contracts SPI-8019116, SPI-8166315, and SPE-8264136. The views and conclusions contained in this document are those of the author and should not be interpreted as representing the official policies, either expressed or implied, of the sponsoring agencies or the United States Government.

Munich, West Germany
June 1987

INTEGRATED NATURAL LANGUAGE DIALOGUE

Chapter 1
Introduction

Natural language dialogue is a continuous, unified phenomenon, not simply a series of unrelated sentences and phrases. Unfortunately, most computational systems for interpreting natural language treat individual utterances as isolated events. A comprehensive computational system for participating in natural language dialogue should be designed so that it can apply a well-integrated set of operations in a uniform fashion, with a continuous context that easily reaches across individual utterances. This work describes such a system, Psli3 (pronounced "sly 3"), and the analysis behind it, concentrating primarily on the computational architecture required for uniform processing of contextual phenomena such as elliptical utterances.

1.1. Ellipsis in natural language

Elliptical utterances are those utterances in which the speaker leaves part of an utterance unsaid, resulting in a phrase that is locally syntactically or semantically incomplete. The hearer is expected to infer the missing portions, either from general knowledge, or, more typically, from the preceding conversational context. Elliptical utterances occur frequently in many kinds of dialogues, including those involving natural language interfaces to data bases, expert systems, and other software packages. They are one of a number of linguistic devices speakers use to simplify individual utterances that depend on the coherence of natural language dialogues. Definite references are another such device touched upon in this work; these allow very short references to objects that are already in the current conversational context. These linguistic devices are used in a highly integrated fashion to produce and comprehend simple, clear utterances based on the conversational context.

Since ellipsis and other dialogue phenomena are so frequent in natural dialogues, it is important for natural language understanding systems to be able to handle them [Carbonell 83]. The users of natural language systems tend to use elliptical utterances even when told not to do so. In addition, these utterances are useful in their own right for the brevity they allow in communication. A system that can interpret these utterances allows the user to communicate more naturally and less self-consciously, as well as allowing shorter utterances for the user to type and the system to interpret. While some earlier methods of understanding elliptical utterances required more time to interpret an elliptical fragment than a full sentence, we feel that elliptical utterances should be easier to interpret than full ones, as is true in our system.

Elliptical utterances can be classified using several kinds of criteria. We have developed a taxonomy based on the type of processing needed in order to interpret, or *resolve*, the elliptical utterance. This is a novel categorization, different from those used by linguists, due to its motivation by the processing constraints discussed in chapters 3, 4, and 5. The first distinction is between elliptical utterances that are resolved based on a previous utterance, or *antecedent*, and those that are resolved using non-linguistic methods. An example of the latter category, a non-antecedent ellipsis, is:

> *Roll call!*

where it is understood from the general context that someone is taking a roll call, and expects other people to respond when their names are stated. Non-antecedent ellipsis is further divided according to whether the utterance can be understood without any reference to the current position in the conversation, as in the example above, or whether the context is used in a non-linguistic way, as in a follow-on to the above command:

    Smith!

which could in general have several interpretations, but here is clearly meant to indicate that the person named Smith should simply indicate his or her presence. An example of the other major category, antecedent ellipsis, is:

    Open the window.
      All the way?
    Half way.

Here the second utterance[1] does not have a clear interpretation without the context provided by the first utterance. Similarly, the third utterance depends on the preceding conversational context for interpretation. Elliptical utterances that have an antecedent are classified as either *intrasentential* or *intersentential*, depending on whether the antecedent is in the current sentence or a previous one. We are only concerned here with the richer and more common of the two classes: intersentential ellipsis. These in turn can be further classified as being either *coreferential* with their antecedents or *non-coreferential*. The example above is coreferential, since exactly the same physical action is being referred to. In the example

    Open the window.
    Now the door.

the utterances are non-coreferential, since they refer to two different actions. The entire taxonomy is illustrated with examples in figure 1-1, and is explored in detail in chapter 3.

---

[1]Throughout this work, indenting a quoted utterance indicates that it is spoken by the other speaker.

- **Non-antecedent ellipsis**

  - **Context-free/Task-dependent**—While sitting at a dinner table: *Salt?*

  - **Context-dependent**—In response to the above request: *Empty!*

- **Antecedent ellipsis**

  - **Non-coreferential**

    - **Reformulation**—A parent speaking to a child: *Please wash your hands.*
      When child returns: *Show me your hands. The other side.*

  - **Coreferential**

    - **Elaboration**—A parent again: *Please clean up your room.*
      As child continues to walk towards the door: *Before you go out to play.*

    - **Correction**—A customer in a restaurant: *I'll have the salmon steak.*
      The waitress: *I wouldn't.* The customer again: *The tuna sandwich.*

    - **Echo**—Another customer: *I'll have a cup of chowder.*
      The waitress: *Chowder?* The customer: *Chowder.*

Figure 1-1:   Our processing taxonomy of dialogue ellipsis

1.2. Ellipsis in natural language interfaces

The two main lines of previous work on ellipsis resolution are the one within semantic grammar systems [Hendrix 77] and the one within case frame based parsing [Carbonell 83]. The work in the semantic grammar paradigm requires a separate style of parsing for elliptical inputs, bottom-up rather than top-down, and has a number of problems associated with its reliance on establishing identity between the syntactic form of the elliptical utterance and that of its antecedent. The case frame based technique is more flexible and general, since it relies on semantic unification of the representations of the ellipsis and antecedent. The case frame method has been extended and incorporated in a more integrated form in the handling of ellipsis in this work. This and other relevant previous work will be discussed in chapter 2.

Previous computational approaches to ellipsis resolution have dealt only with reformulation of previous requests by the same speaker. Our Psli3 system takes advantage of the uniformity and integration of its design to handle several other conversational situations in addition to reformulation, such as cross-speaker ellipsis. Figures 1-2, 1-3, and 1-4 give an example of a dialogue fragment that this system can handle; the current domain of the system is information retrieval from a medical database. No other system can handle the range of ellipsis phenomena handled in Psli3, nor is any approach as uniform and extensible, since they all require special-purpose mechanisms.

The first pair of utterances in figures 1-2, 1-3, and 1-4 shows a typical reformulation ellipsis, where a second query is produced by modifying the first. The next interaction shows the system generating a question to resolve a failed reference, and interpreting the elliptical answer. Then there is an elliptical utterance where the missing part is a constituent rather than the more common missing superstructure. The last two interactions show how the system can interpret multiple part utterances in different ways: the first is taken to be a clarification of a single requested action, while the second is taken to be a reformulation resulting in two requested actions. The general design of the system is described briefly below, and details of its internal function are provided in chapter 4.

Show me some ribs.
>   RIB_NUMBER_7
>   (IS-A (VALUE TRUE_RIB))
>
>   RIB_NUMBER_6
>   (IS-A (VALUE TRUE_RIB))
>
>   RIB_NUMBER_5
>   (IS-A (VALUE TRUE_RIB))

Some other ribs.
<Comment: Understanding the semantics of "other" is
    required.>
>   RIB_NUMBER_4
>   (IS-A (VALUE TRUE_RIB))
>
>   RIB_NUMBER_3
>   (IS-A (VALUE TRUE_RIB))
>
>   RIB_NUMBER_2
>   (IS-A (VALUE TRUE_RIB))

Display the irregular bones.
<Comment: Definite reference without a referent requires
    clarification interaction.

Both parties use ellipsis.>
>   **WHICH IRREGULAR BONES?**

Any irregular bones.
>   ETHMOID
>   (IS-A (VALUE IRREGULAR_BONE))
>   (PART-OF (VALUE CRANIUM))
>
>   HYOID
>   (IS-A (VALUE IRREGULAR_BONE))
>   (BILATERAL (VALUE F))
>   (LOCATED-IN (VALUE NECK))
>
>   INCUS
>   (IS-A (VALUE IRREGULAR_BONE))
>   (LOCATED-IN (VALUE HEAD))

Figure 1-2:   Example dialogue with Psli3 (first third)

Show Mark.
<Comment: Syntactically ambiguous, but not semantically.>
>
> **ETHMOID**
> **(IS-A (VALUE IRREGULAR_BONE))**
> **(PART-OF (VALUE CRANIUM))**
>
> **HYOID**
> **(IS-A (VALUE IRREGULAR_BONE))**
> **(BILATERAL (VALUE F))**
> **(LOCATED-IN (VALUE NECK))**
>
> **INCUS**
> **(IS-A (VALUE IRREGULAR_BONE))**
> **(LOCATED-IN (VALUE HEAD))**

Display some sternal ribs. To Phil.
<Comment: Two actions are merged into one.>
>
> **RIB_NUMBER_7**
> **(IS-A (VALUE TRUE_RIB))**
>
> **RIB_NUMBER_6**
> **(IS-A (VALUE TRUE_RIB))**
>
> **RIB_NUMBER_5**
> **(IS-A (VALUE TRUE_RIB))**

Figure 1-3: Example dialogue with Psli3 (second third)

1.3. Computational architecture

We first describe our general approach to understanding elliptical utterances, and then explain the architecture within which we have implemented our system. The processing of an elliptical utterance begins when the system encounters an input it cannot interpret as a complete sentence. Conceptually, there are four steps in the process:

- **Recognize the elliptical fragment**—The system must decide that the input is an elliptical fragment, as opposed to a spelling error or extragrammatical utterance.

Display some asternal ribs. Some flat bones.

<Comment: Two actions are left separate due to case role
conflict.>

       RIB_NUMBER_9
       (IS-A (VALUE FALSE_RIB))

       RIB_NUMBER_8
       (IS-A (VALUE FALSE_RIB))

       RIB_NUMBER_10
       (IS-A (VALUE FALSE_RIB))

       VOMER
       (IS-A (VALUE FLAT_BONE))
       (PART-OF (VALUE FACE))
       (BILATERAL (VALUE T))

       STERNUM
       (IS-A (VALUE FLAT_BONE))
       (BILATERAL (VALUE F))
       (LOCATED-IN (VALUE TRUNK))

       SCAPULA
       (JOINED-BY (VALUE SHOULDER_JOINT))
       (IS-A (VALUE FLAT_BONE))
       (LOCATED-IN (VALUE SHOULDER TRUNK))
       (BILATERAL (VALUE T))

Figure 1-4:   Example dialogue with Psli3 (conclusion)

- **Match the antecedent**—The antecedent of the elliptical
  fragment must be identified. This is generally the preceding
  utterance, which may have been uttered by either speaker.

- **Instantiate the new full utterance**—The antecedent and the
  elliptical utterance must be merged. This is where the case frame
  based ellipsis resolution technique is used.

- **Determine the intended effect**—The communicative purpose
  of the utterance must be ascertained. This is done using the type
  of case frame match, any reference relationship that exists
  between the utterances, and the conversational context.

Processing can then continue as it would with a full sentence.

The system has been implemented in a *production system language*. The term *production system language* is used here to mean a programming language in which the program, or *production system*, consists of a large number of *production rules*. These rules each specify one or more actions that should be taken when a specified set of conditions occur. The conditions are expressed in the rule's left hand side, and the actions in the right hand side. The state of the system is stored in one or more *working memories*, each of which is normally an unordered set of *working memory elements*. It is the working memory that the conditions test, and that the actions modify, in addition to doing input and output. The language's actual execution is carried out by a production system interpreter, which tests the rules against the current state of the system, determines which rules have their left hand sides satisfied, and then selects one or more rules and executes their right hand sides. This repeats in a cycle, as long as the system is running. The specific production system language we have used, OPS5, will be discussed in some detail in section 4.2.

One of the reasons we chose to use a production system architecture is that we feel it is easier to design a natural language dialogue system that follows roughly how human beings handle natural language dialogue. Such a strategy allows one to use intuitions about how dialogue works. Also, the system will be talking with human beings, so at some level it is necessary to track the course of thought of its conversational partner. Production systems are widely used for cognitive modelling in cognitive psychology, and so are an obvious choice. A production system engaging in dialogue naturally appears to be carrying out a single, continuous event. The production rules respond to an input by creating data structures in working memory that represent its understanding of the input, respond to the existence of this structure by generating goals representing decisions about what to do next, and then respond to these goals by generating the representation of an output in working memory, which then causes other rules to actually produce an output. All of these data structures persist in working memory for some length of time after the input and output actions, and are thus naturally available as a context for further input understanding or decision making. This system is by far the most extensive work to date on building an actual natural language interface in a true production system.

Another reason we have used a production system architecture is to allow a high degree of integration among different kinds of operations in a uniform environment. Because there is no fixed control structure, rules containing knowledge about parsing natural language input, natural language semantics, the domain lexicon, domain knowledge base access, ellipsis resolution, error repair, and other types of knowledge can interact in a highly integrated fashion, bringing their knowledge to bear wherever it is needed. The domain knowledge base is a separate entity from the production system, and is an unmodified copy of a pre-existing medical knowledge base built for another project. There is a set of productions that accesses it on demand, not only to retrieve information in response to user requests, but also to carry out semantics checks on proposed interpretations of those requests, locate referents of noun phrases that requires domain-dependent class membership knowledge, and to look up frame names that are not in the lexicon. This shows that it is not necessary to place all the declarative knowledge in a production system in the production system's rules. In contrast, lexicon entries are compiled into production rules at system start-up time from lexicon frames in the knowledge base. This prevents the system from having to search through all the lexicon frames at run-time to find the entries for the words in the input.

The lack of a fixed control structure also allows new rules to make use of old rules that are already present in an additive way. If there are already rules that elaborate a particular structure, a new rule only has to create this structure, and the others will automatically elaborate it. Adding new variations of existing features is made quite easy; the rule for handling elaboration ellipsis (page 91) was written and debugged in less than one day, even though it involved creating a small set of case role conflict checking rules. This added a whole new category of ellipsis to the system's capabilities.

The technique we use to interpret natural language within this architecture is called *semantic chart parsing*. It is based on chart parsing, adapted to fit the production system approach and to allow semantic, as well as syntactic, information in its states and rules. The technique, and the data structures it generates, fit the production system architecture well, and contribute to the smooth integration of different functions. It also extends naturally to form multiple-sentence charts, so that where several sentences are closely related they can be interpreted as a single entity. The simple natural language generation capabilities of the system are designed to use the same internal data structures as the chart, which also enhances the system's integration. These features are all explained in great detail in chapters 4 and 5.

1.4. Outline of the book

This first chapter has been an overview of the whole project. Chapter 2 reviews the relevant prior work in ellipsis resolution, dialogue modelling, and chart parsing. Chapter 3 gives an analysis of ellipsis and other dialogue phenomena that the system incorporates. Chapter 4 describes in detail the system as it has been implemented, with example rules, data structures, and traces. Chapter 5 presents a fine-grained, annotated trace of the system interpreting a sequence of four utterances. The final chapter, number 6, contains our conclusions about this effort and suggestions for future work.

Chapter 2
Relevant Previous Work

Here we review previous work related to the current project, and indicate how it compares with our work. The three areas examined are ellipsis resolution, dialogue modelling, and chart parsing.

2.1. Work on ellipsis resolution

Two main lines of research on understanding elliptical utterances have been undertaken. The first occurred in the context of semantic grammar parsing systems, beginning with Hendrix's LADDER system [Hendrix 77] and continuing with the SOPHIE [Burton 75] and PLANES [Waltz 77] systems. The other previous effort began more recently with Carbonell's DYPAR-II system [Carbonell 83] and has continued with DYPAR-IV and PLUME[TM] [Cellio 84].

2.1.1. Semantic grammar ellipsis resolution

This technique in its initial form consisted of parsing an unrecognizable fragment bottom-up as a non-terminal in the semantic grammar, and then replacing the part of the previous parse tree corresponding to the same non-terminal with the new elliptical parse tree. Not only did this require a different parsing strategy for ellipsis than for full utterances, since normal parsing was top-down, but this method was very sensitive to quirks in the construction of the grammar, since the use or non-use of a non-terminal in a grammar rule would affect whether or not a certain class of ellipsis could be handled. Some classes simply could not be handled at all, such as elliptical utterances consisting of several disjoint nonterminals, and those where the syntactic form of the elliptical utterance did not match that of its antecedent.

The following example illustrates the first problem. In order to handle the phrase *disk with two ports*, a semantic grammar could include a more complex version of either of the following two grammar fragments:

```
<disk> --> <disk> <prep> <disk-property>
```

```
<disk> --> <disk> <prep-disk-property>
<prep-disk-property> --> <prep> <disk-property>
```

where the non-terminals <disk>, <prep>, and <disk-property> can expand to the words *disk*, *with*, and *two ports*, respectively. Using the original LADDER algorithm, the elliptical utterance *With two ports* could only be handled using the second grammar fragment. If the first grammar were used, the phrase in question would not correspond to any single non-terminal.

This method was later improved somewhat by allowing an elliptical utterance to match a sequence of non-terminals that occurred in a contiguous segment of a grammar rule, thus producing a set of possible replacements corresponding to a larger set of non-terminals than the specifically defined ones. Using this stronger version, the example above could be handled using either of the grammar fragments, since with the first, it would correspond to a contiguous pair of non-terminals. This also solved the most common forms of the problem of elliptical utterances consisting of several truly disjoint pieces. It still could not handle situations where the elliptical utterance had a different syntactic form from the antecedent.

The SOPHIE system [Burton 75] and the PLANES system [Waltz 77] each included the weaker form of this algorithm within a semantic grammar type system.

2.1.2. Case frame ellipsis resolution

The DYPAR [Carbonell 83] and PLUME^{TM} [Cellio 84] parsers combine case frame and semantic grammar techniques, using the semantic grammar style of pattern matching to match the input string to a case frame grammar. Case frame grammars specify which case frame representations of natural language inputs are allowable for this domain. These representations consist of nested structures of case frames, each of which has a *header* indicating what type of case frame it is, and an unordered set of *cases*, each with a case name and a *filler*, which is either another case frame, a special symbol, or a number. The ellipsis resolution is done at the case frame level, allowing a more fine-grained and less syntactic matching of the ellipsis to the antecedent. This solves the following problem. Given the example:

> *Show me all fixed pack disks with two ports.*
> *Disks with one port.*

the semantic grammar ellipsis resolution technique would produce a non-terminal corresponding to <disk>, so that the phrase *disks with one port* would replace the entire phrase *fixed pack disks with two ports*. However, the intended reference is to *fixed pack disks with one port*, requiring a finer-grained division of the semantic components of the phrase. In addition, although different syntactic forms of an ellipsis, such as *single port* vs. *with one port*, should not affect the outcome, a semantic grammar approach will handle them differently, since they must correspond to different non-terminals in a context-free grammar.

The case frame ellipsis resolution technique avoids both these problems, due to its more detailed, more purely semantic internal representation. In this technique, the antecedent utterance and the elliptical fragment are merged by taking the antecedent, overwriting any of its cases that are present in the ellipsis with the fillers from the ellipsis, retaining any of the antecedent's cases that are not present in the ellipsis, and adding any new cases present only in the ellipsis. In some versions of this system, replacement of the case header causes wholesale replacement of all its subcomponents, whereas in other versions, only those subcomponents that are incompatible with the new head are replaced.

2.1.3. PSLI3 ellipsis resolution

All of these systems have been restricted to understanding an elliptical utterance that refers to a previous utterance by the user, as opposed to one that refers to an utterance generated by the system, and all have used a combination of syntax and semantics. The first similarity is due no doubt to the lack of a suitable internal representation of the system's output, while the second is due to the necessity of using both sources of information to achieve any kind of reasonable results.

Ellipsis resolution in our system essentially follows the DYPAR approach, recast into the production system framework. A more recent version of the DYPAR system uses a modified version of the KAFKA [Mauldin 84] rule-based case frame transformation system to carry out the ellipsis resolution, so that its ellipsis resolution is fairly similar to ours, except that the control of the conversational situations in which ellipsis would be attempted is still in Lisp, and is restricted to reformulation ellipsis (see chapter 3). Using a production system allows more flexibility to be built into the system relatively easily, so that ellipses in other conversational situations can be handled; for example, in responses to questions, or in multiple-part utterances where follow-on sentences are elliptical. Additionally, ambiguity and possibly complex semantic checking are easily handled through a combination of the production system architecture and chart representations (see section 2.3). While such features could probably be added to any of these systems, they fit in naturally and easily with the production system approach, as we have demonstrated in our Psli3 implementation (see chapter 4).

2.2. Work on dialogue modelling

The topic of dialogue modelling has included a wide variety of approaches to the problem of handling natural language interactions at levels beyond the individual sentence. These range from concrete systems for handling specific discourse phenomena [Sidner 79, Grosz 77] to more abstract attempts to handle higher-order effects [Allen 80, Reichman 85].

2.2.1. Syntactic focusing in discourse

In her work on comprehending definite anaphora in discourse [Sidner 79], Sidner defines a computational model for focus shifting. The current, former, and potential foci determine how objects can be referenced; the type of reference actually used, such as pronominalization, changes what is in focus and what is available as a potential focus. Several variables, lists, and a *focus stack* are used to keep track of which phrases are available as focused objects in different situations. A rule-based algorithm is presented for calculating the current focus at any point in the discourse, and other rules are presented for determining what different types of references refer to.

Although this is probably the best work yet on general, concrete discourse phenomena, it does have some problems. While the rules presented cover many cases, they clearly do not handle all relevant situations[2]. It has not been shown that this approach can be extended to correctly cover all cases. From our point of view, the main problem with this approach is that it is somewhat too syntactic; while semantics are used, they take a second place to the syntactic focus mechanisms.

While the discourses examined in Sidner's work are single speaker, it is likely that the rules for focus shift could be adapted to a dialogue context. The main change involved in incorporating them into a system such as ours, other than placing more emphasis on semantics, would be to replace the special-purpose data structures for handling focus shift with the use of data structures that already exist in working memory. In other words, in a system based on a production system architecture, rather than having special data structures that exist solely for handling linguistic focus shifts, the structures already existing in working memory would simply be accessed as variables, lists, or stacks, depending on the rules used to access them. For instance, in our system definite references make a stack-like use of possible referents, while the different cases in a single antecedent case frame are treated in a list-like way by the ellipsis resolution rules. These differences are not implemented by any special data structures, but simply by the manner in which the productions in question are written. This is presented in detail in chapter 4.

---

[2]Donald Kosy (personal communication) found a number of unresolved problems in applying them to the reading of an accounting textbook.

2.2.2. Task-oriented focusing in dialogue

Another real system that deals with surface linguistic phenomena is Grosz's work on focus in task-oriented dialogues [Grosz 77]. Here *focus spaces* are defined, using contexts that are part of the semantic network representation of the task to be accomplished, in the main example the assembly of a pump. The focus spaces are ordered hierarchically, and the system tracks its conversational partner as the dialogue goes from one subtask to another. Objects in the current focus space or its parent can be referred to using definite references, and references by the participants to objects in other focus spaces are used to indicate when the dialogue moves on to a new subtask. This type of focusing is at a larger grain than the focusing described by Sidner.

Grosz points out that these techniques are most applicable to dialogues where there is some task structure available. In the database access dialogues she examined, there did not appear to be a useful task structure on which to base a division into focus spaces. If our system were to be applied to a domain with significant task structure, this type of focusing could be incorporated through the loading of frames from the semantic network into working memory, and their subsequent deletion when the corresponding subtask was no longer relevant. The current system loads frames into working memory, as will be described in chapter 4, but there is no provision for deleting a context; the system cannot forget anything during an execution.

2.2.3. Formal discourse representation

There has been a fair amount of work on formal semantics for natural language, including that of Appelt [Appelt 82] and Barwise and Perry [Barwise 83]. The formal discourse work by Webber [Webber 78] concentrates on formally representing all the objects generated by the current sentence that could possibly be referents of future utterances, through the use of an extension of first-order predicate logic. This extension involves the use of restricted quantification, lambda-abstraction, and some new operators. There is also a special predicate **evoke** S, x that indicates that x is the description evoked by an utterance S, and not a different one of the same form.

While it is important to have a precise characterization of the phenomena one wishes to handle for design purposes, it is not at all clear that first-order predicate calculus is an adequate representation for natural language, even from a purely logical point of view [Barwise 83]. From a computational point of view, the data structures used are often at least as important as the logical statements they correspond to. Still, it is interesting to note that the **evoke** predicate corresponds closely to the use of a unique object ID in our system.

2.2.4. Speech acts and dialogue modelling

In their work on planning and speech acts [Allen 80], Allen and Perrault attempt to recognize a speaker's underlying plans, and use that information to produce helpful responses. They attempt to infer the speaker's plan from his actions, reasoning about his beliefs and desires. One of their desired results is the ability to recognize the intentions behind elliptical utterances. In the example they give, a person goes up to the information booth at a train station, and asks

> *The train to Windsor?*

to which the person in the booth replies

> *It leaves at 3:15 from gate 7*

Their system goes through a plan inference process to deduce that there are two possible things the first speaker might need to know, and then generates the answer to both.

Even in the very limited domain they have chosen, plan inference is a hard problem, and their reasoning process uses a variety of heuristics to reduce its search. Since their planning process uses task-dependent information in its search heuristics already, it would seem simpler to provide the system with information about what a user would want to know about particular trains. This could conceivably be stored knowledge that was produced off-line by a reasoning process such as the one they describe. On-line reasoning about plans would only really be necessary in very unusual cases, although it might be easier simply to ask the user what is wanted. The main point here is that plan inference is in general too difficult to carry out on-line, and therefore it is probably not often invoked in the course of ordinary dialogue.

As we describe in chapter 3, task-dependent ellipsis requires a different type of processing than the linguistically-oriented ellipses with which we are concerned. If a computationally feasible method of inferring user plans were found, it certainly would be useful in handling this type of ellipsis. But where our methods are applicable, they are much more efficient.

2.2.5. Discourse grammar

Reichman [Reichman 85] has developed a discourse grammar based on an ATN-like approach to *conversational moves*. Unlike the speech acts approach, these moves are signalled by *clue words* such as **Anyway...** or **But look...**, not by any attempt to deduce speakers' beliefs and plans. The conversational moves correspond to shifts in *context spaces*, which affect such things as whether references can be pronominalized. The different context spaces created during a discourse produce a hierarchical structure. It appears that the system did not actually run on real discourses.

From the discourse grammar she gives, it appears that the discourse structure this system tracks is actually the structure of arguments, since all of her example discourses are adversarial discussions. This makes it similar to the task-oriented system described above, except that the task structure is replaced by a dynamically-built argument structure of supports, counter-claims, and the like. The choice of an ATN-like formalism seems odd, since ATNs are widely considered to be too rigid even for sentential grammar, which is much more structured than discourse. Finally, it seems that there should be a semantic level above clue words and below context space shifts, so that the widely varying phrases that can be used to indicate the conversational relationship of the following utterance could be mapped into a small set of conversational relationship indicators.

Our Psli3 system has one type of conversational move, in the form of an error-repair subdialogue. This is typical for database access applications, where there is no adversarial argument structure or other clear task structure to provide predictable shifts in the dialogue. It is initiated by the system, so there is no mechanism for noticing conversational context shifts.

2.2.6. Dialogue modelling in Psli3

While there has been no explicit effort at dialogue modelling within this system, there is an implicit dialogue model, namely the context provided by case frame structures residing in working memory. These represent both natural language input and output. Together with other data structures built in working memory, such as the frames representing semantic network information, they provide a model of the dialogue processing that has occurred during a run of the system up to the current time. We have indicated in the sections immediately above how this approach could be adapted to provide the functionality of the different types of explicit discourse models that have been proposed.

2.3. Work on chart parsing

Chart parsing was first developed as a syntactic method by Martin Kay [Kay 67, Kay 73] and is explained in Winograd [Winograd 83].

The basic idea is similar to the programming technique known as *dynamic programming*, in that partial results are stored in a data structure indexed by the input, they can subsequently be looked up rather than being recalculated if needed at another point in the calculation, and so no partial result ever needs to be calculated more than once. In parsing systems, this means that the result of applying a rule to a segment of the input, called an *edge*, is stored in a table indexed by the starting and ending positions of the input, and other rules looking for constituents of this type check the table rather than building it again. In *active chart parsing*, first developed by Earley [Earley 70], the process is controlled in such a way as to parse at optimal speed for unrestricted context-free grammars. This is achieved by incrementally matching the syntactic rules, and storing partial matches in the chart as *active edges*. A new technique called MLR [Tomita 85], which adapts LR parsing to handle any context-free grammar, can be looked on as an improvement on active chart parsing, in that it has a much smaller constant factor on the same optimal parsing time.

In our early work on parsing inside a production system [Frederking 85], the main problem we had was to handle the ambiguity inherent in natural languages, while trying to build structures that were largely semantic. Backtracking with semantic structures is difficult, especially in a production system, and maintaining multiple parallel parses became prohibitively expensive in terms of time and space. Adapting the chart parser to the production system framework solved this problem in an elegant way.

Chart parsing also provided the additional benefit of separating the state of the parse from its control structure. In many parsers, part of the state of a parse is hidden in the control state of the program. In chart-based systems,

all of the state can be placed in the chart, allowing the system to be
recursively called on a new input while in the middle of a parse, or allowing
it to use complex control strategies, without major difficulties. We call our
approach *semantic chart parsing* to emphasize the presence of semantics in
the states representing constituents, and in the rules that build and match
them. This method corresponds to a simple chart parser rather than an
active chart parser, as will be explained in chapter 4.

A technique reported by Jardine and Shebs [Jardine 83] appears to function
in a similar fashion, although it was developed by adding parallelism to
PHRAN [Wilensky 80], and is not integrated into a uniform production
system. It builds up semantic descriptions of phrases in the input to form a
partially ordered set of concepts. A concept that covers the whole input is a
correct interpretation of the input. Intermediate concepts function as they
do in a chart, allowing constituents to be built only once at any given
location in the input.

2.4. How Psli3 differs from other systems

In understanding the advantages of Psli3 over other types of systems, the
key is the uniformity in architecture that allows an unprecedented
integration of the different features of a natural language system[3]:

- Rule-based, case frame ellipsis resolution is implemented within a
  uniform architecture, allowing ellipsis to be resolved in a variety
  of conversational situations without any great increase in
  program complexity. Different types of ellipsis resolution
  naturally act in a compositional fashion.

- The several kinds of dialogue phenomena that are handled are
  represented and dealt with in a uniform way. Definite reference
  is implemented naturally, as is ellipsis resolution. Both of these
  integrate smoothly with clarificational sub-dialogues, which is the
  only form of conversational structure in the system. If there were
  a task structure, conversational contexts could be handled by the
  presence or absence of semantic network frames in working
  memory, which are already used by the current system.

---

[3]For details on all of this, see chapter 4.

- Semantic chart parsing blends in well with the uniform architecture. It allows easy, clear handling of ambiguity, and incremental semantic checking of both full and elliptical utterances. Its lack of hidden state simplifies the handling of any complex conversational situations that might occur.

Chapter 3
An Analysis of
Natural Language Dialogue

This book presents a view of dialogue as an ongoing, continuous action involving two participants, rather than as a series of separate actions by one participant. In preparation for understanding how intersentential ellipsis and other dialogue phenomena can be understood from this point of view, this chapter analyzes these phenomena on the basis of what type of processing they require.

3.1. An Analysis of intersentential ellipsis

As was mentioned in the introductory chapter, elliptical utterances that depend on the preceding conversation are classified as either *intrasentential* or *intersentential*, depending on whether the *antecedent* utterance, which supplies the missing part, is in the current sentence or a previous one. We will only be looking at intersentential ellipsis, since this is more frequent in the short sentences typical of discourse, and since the same intersentential ellipsis resolution techniques—with added syntactic constraints—seem to apply to intrasentential ellipsis in its most frequent form: coordinate clauses. For example, the conjoined sentence

Give the apple to John and the grapefruit to Mary.

would seem to be processed in essentially the same way as the pair of utterances

Give the apple to John.
The grapefruit to Mary.

A system that can process elliptical utterances allows greater brevity in communication than one that cannot, especially in terms of correcting and modifying previous utterances, but it also must have greater inferential capabilities.

3.1.1. Top-level taxonomy of intersentential ellipsis

We have divided intersentential ellipsis into two major categories, each with two subcategories, based on the processing required to understand the ellipsis. These are:

- Non-antecedent ellipsis

  o Context-free/Task-dependent

  o Context-dependent

- Antecedent ellipsis

  o Coreferential

  o Non-coreferential

The two major categories differ in whether there is an antecedent for the ellipsis. This difference determines how the ellipsis will be resolved into a full utterance. In those ellipses without antecedents, the missing portion must come from either general knowledge or the current situation. As an example of context-free or task-dependent non-antecedent ellipsis, suppose, in a natural language interface for a computer operating system, a user types:

Disk quota?

The system should be able to decide, without any conversational context, that an elliptical question about disk quotas can only mean that the user wants to know what his disk quota is, because of the task that the system is designed to carry out. While task-dependent knowledge differs from truly context-free knowledge, this distinction does not matter from our point of view. In contrast, if the user would then type:

The other disk?

the system would need to use the context of the previous action to understand that the user wants the quota of the other disk, and not the number of files on it, for instance. This is context-dependent, but still does not need to use a linguistic antecedent to provide the missing parts. We are not treating any of these non-antecedent types in any detail, since the processing required is not particularly linguistic in nature, but concerns general issues of flexibility and context awareness.

We are primarily concerned with antecedent ellipsis. The two subcategories of antecedent ellipsis are those that are coreferential with their antecedents, and those that are not. By "coreferential", we mean that the two utterances refer to the same exact real-world instance of an action or object. Such an instance is represented in any reasonable computational system by a unique individual data structure, so that it is possible to have two separate instances of an action with exactly the same case frame description, but existing as separate data structures. Although most computational systems assume that each utterance refers to a new action, it seems that sentences should be taken to be coreferential unless there is a reason to believe they are not. That is, if two utterances do have identical case frame structures, or even have compatible structures, and it is possible for them to corefer, then they do. If, however, we know that they cannot corefer, either due to conflicting fillers of the same case, explicit markers such as *other* or *again*, or from pragmatic considerations, as illustrated below, then their referents are distinct actions, represented as distinct data structures.

An example of coreferential ellipsis, in a computer equipment ordering system, is:

Give me a large disk.
    With two ports?

While *With two ports?* does not corefer with any part of the antecedent, the elliptical verb phrase produced when it is resolved does. This verb phrase consists of the antecedent sentence plus the new prepositional phrase, which modifies the noun phrase that is the object of the verb phrase, followed by a question mark. The verb phrase in this new sentence refers to the same giving action as the first sentence, asking if it should be extended in the suggested way. As an example of a non-coreferential ellipsis, suppose a user of a medical information system types:

Show me a flat bone.

and then after the requested information is displayed types:

Another flat bone.
This second input does not corefer with the noun phrase in the first input,
since *another* explicitly means one other than the antecedent. The second
input's elliptical verb phrase does not corefer with the antecedent's verb
phrase, since its antecedent refers to an action that at this point has already
been carried out, and one cannot request an action that has already taken
place. This demonstrates that non-coreference can be determined by
pragmatic considerations.

3.1.2. Understanding elliptical utterances

The steps in interpreting an elliptical utterance are shown in figure 3-1.
The process begins when an input fails to be parsed as a complete sentence.
The system must decide that the input is a possible ellipsis, and not an
ungrammatical fragment due to a spelling or grammar error. This can be
done by recognizing it as a type of fragment that the system knows how to
interpret as an elliptical utterance.

Recognize input as elliptical fragment

Match possible antecedent

Instantiate new full utterance

Determine intended effect

Figure 3-1:   Steps in understanding an elliptical utterance

The next step is to find a matching antecedent. This is usually the
preceding sentence, which may have been uttered by the current speaker or
generated by the system. It must contain a constituent similar to the current
one, or else be able to accept the current utterance as an extension. The
different possible types of structural match will be reviewed below.

Once an antecedent is located, the current ellipsis can be instantiated into a
full utterance using the antecedent as its context. This can be done using a
variant of the DYPAR/PLUME^{TM} technique described in the preceding
chapter. Further parsing may be involved, in that the meaning of a
preposition introducing an elliptical prepositional phrase may not be clear
until the sentence it attaches to is known. Since, in a production system
implementation, the whole structure of the antecedent utterance is still

present in working memory, it does not need to be copied in order to produce the instantiation. A unique identification of the antecedent, and how the ellipsis is related to it, suffices.

Finally, once the elliptical utterance is fully instantiated, the intended effect of the utterance must be determined. This is also discussed below.

The structures used here to represent natural language input and output are *case frame* structures. As mentioned in the previous chapter, these consist of a nested structure of case frames, each of which has a *header* indicating what type of case frame it is, and an unordered set of *cases*, each with a case name and a *filler*, which is either another case frame, a special symbol, or a number. Case frame structures are a natural way to represent the structure of human language, and are widely used, both in natural language processing [Carbonell 83, Cellio 84, Hayes 86, Birnbaum 81, Waltz 77] and, in somewhat different and less domain-dependent forms, in linguistics [Bresnan 82, Jackendoff 83].

In matching an elliptical utterance to its antecedent, then, we are matching two case frame structures. There are three kinds of structural match between elliptical utterances and their antecedents:

- **Replacement**—The elliptical utterance replaces the corresponding part of the antecedent:

    Display a large disk drive.
    A large tape drive.

  A simple case frame representation for this pair of utterances is shown in figures 3-2 and 3-3, below.

- **Repetition**—The elliptical utterance repeats the corresponding part:

    Display a large disk.
    A large disk?

- **Extension**—The elliptical utterance extends the antecedent, by attaching to it as a new component in a previously unfilled case:

    Display a large disk.
    With dual heads.

Combinations of these three kinds of match also occur. For instance, the example of replacement above includes some repetition as well.

To review, the DYPAR/PLUME[TM] ellipsis instantiation algorithm is based
on case frame matching. To instantiate the full new utterance, one takes a
copy of the antecedent and replaces any shared cases, retains any old cases
not present in the new utterance, and adds any new cases not present in the
old one. This process is illustrated in figures 3-2 through 3-4, using the
previous replacement example.

```
[Action
    action: Display
    object:
        [Object
            det: Indefinite
            head: Disk-drive
            size: Large]]
```

Figure 3-2:   Case frame diagram for antecedent:
Display a large disk drive.

```
[Object
    det: Indefinite
    head: Tape-drive
    size: Large]]
```

Figure 3-3:   Case frame diagram for elliptical utterance:
A large tape drive.

```
[Action
    action: Display
    object:
        [Object
            det: Indefinite
            head: Tape-drive
            size: Large]]
```

Figure 3-4:   Case frame diagram for resolved utterance

One problematic issue is what to do with subordinate cases when a case
header is replaced. In some situations it appears that any old cases that still
make sense semantically are kept, whereas in others it seems that wholesale
deletion of subordinate cases takes place. It may be that domain semantics
or pragmatic considerations determine which course of action is followed. In
this vein, we have discovered at least one case of what appears to be an
intersentential syntactic constraint, in that an elliptical noun phrase without
a quantifier or determiner retains the quantifier and determiner of the
corresponding noun phrase in its antecedent, whereas one with a quantifier or
determiner does not. That is, in the pair of utterances

Display a long bone.

Irregular bone.

the elliptical utterance should be interpreted as *Display an irregular bone*, while in

Display every long bone.
Irregular bone.

the elliptical utterance should be *Display every irregular bone.* In contrast, either pair with *An irregular bone* as the elliptical utterance should be interpreted as *Display an irregular bone.* Alternatively, this could be looked at as an instance of the replaced-header problem discussed above, which is semantic in nature, but has syntactic consequences.

Determining the intended effect of an antecedent elliptical utterance requires the consideration of a combination of the case frame match described above and any reference relationship between the two utterances:

- **Reformulation**—If the two utterances do not corefer, the elliptical utterance is a reformulation, that is, it is a new sentence that simply shares some repeated structure that has already been communicated:

   Give me a dual ported disk drive.
   A tape drive.

   As was previously mentioned, this non-coreference can sometimes be determined pragmatically.

- **Correction**—If the two utterances do corefer, then the type of match between them comes into play. If a replacement corefers, this indicates a correction of an error, since the ellipsis refers to the same thing in a different way. In the example:

   Give me a dual ported tape drive.
   Dual ported disk drive?

   the second utterance can be resolved as *Give you a dual ported disk drive?*, that is, offering a tentative replacement for the first speaker's utterance. As seen in this example, the speaker may echo surrounding parts of the antecedent to help establish where the replacement should go.

- **Question answer**—This is the only case we know of where conversational context comes into play. If the ellipsis corefers with an antecedent that is a questioned noun phrase, then the ellipsis is taken to be an elliptical answer to that question:

> *Dual ported tape drive?*
> *Dual ported disk drive.*

This is a sub-type of correction ellipsis. It is distinguished here because the strong expectation of an answer to a question makes the determination of which case is being replaced trivial.

- **Elaboration**—If the second utterance extends and corefers with the first, then it is an elaboration, that is, the antecedent utterance is made more specific by explicitly providing additional information that is either new or was assumed before:

  > *Give me a dual ported disk drive. With blue*
  > *indicator lights.*

- **Echo**—If the two utterances corefer and the second merely repeats a portion of the first, then the ellipsis is an echo. The echoed portion has been repeated in order to confirm that it is correct:

  > *Give me a dual ported tape drive.*
  > *Dual ported tape drive?*

These rules seem to work for full sentences as well as ellipses, raising a possible resolution to the phenomenon of extended case frames, where several full sentences are used to describe a single event:

> *John swung the hammer around his head.*
> *He swung it right into my stereo.*

This pair of sentences refers to a single event, with the second extending the first, making the pair an elaboration, in the same way as the pair:

> *John swung the hammer around his head.*
> *Right into my stereo.*

So these intended effect categories may apply to full sentences as well as elliptical ones.

The full processing taxonomy we have developed here is summarized in figure 3-5, which was already presented in the first chapter. This shows that there are four major categories of antecedent ellipsis for a natural language system to understand. While further sub-divisions are possible, they do not affect the general type of processing for the utterance.

For example, a further sub-division in terms of the structure of the

- **Non-antecedent ellipsis**

  - ○ **Context-free/Task-dependent**—While sitting at a dinner table: *Salt?*

  - ○ **Context-dependent**—In response to the above request: *Empty!*

- **Antecedent ellipsis**

  - ○ **Non-coreferential**

    - **Reformulation**—A parent speaking to a child: *Please wash your hands.*
      When child returns: *Show me your hands. The other side.*

  - ○ **Coreferential**

    - **Elaboration**—A parent again: *Please clean up your room.*
      As child continues to walk towards the door: *Before you go out to play.*

    - **Correction**—A customer in a restaurant: *I'll have the salmon steak.*
      The waitress: *I wouldn't.* The customer again: *The tuna sandwich.*

    - **Echo**—Another customer: *I'll have a cup of chowder.*
      The waitress: *Chowder?* The customer: *Chowder.*

Figure 3-5: Our processing taxonomy of dialogue ellipsis

elliptical utterance itself is used in this work. In a system based on the case frame approach to language, such as this one, full sentences are made up of *clausal* (verb phrase) case frames and *nominal* (noun phrase) case frames. Each of these can be involved in two major types of ellipsis: the elision of the head of the case frame and some of its cases, and the elision of a subordinate

case of a case frame. The first can be called *functional ellipsis*, because the
function of the remaining phrase in the original case frame is left
undetermined, while the second can be referred to as *constituent ellipsis*,
because a constituent part of the case frame is elided [Shopen 72].

This produces a description of an elliptical utterance in terms of four
structural categories, shown here with their elided parts in italics. Both
nominal examples are also clausal functional ellipsis:

- **Clausal Functional**—Utterances such as *Show me A tape
  drive.*

- **Clausal Constituent**—Utterances such as *Show John the tape
  drive.*

- **Nominal Functional**—Utterances such as *Show me Another
  tape drive.*

- **Nominal Constituent**—Utterances such as *Show me every
  tape drive.*

Although this classification will prove useful in discussing rule-based ellipsis
resolution, it does not affect the general type of processing applied to an
utterance. These are merely syntactic differences in the form of the
utterance. All the examples used in this list, for example, can be produced as
reformulation ellipses, by having the elliptical utterance follow an antecedent
it is not coreferent with:

   Show me a disk drive.
   A tape drive.

Or they can be produced as correction ellipses, by having the elliptical
utterance follow an antecedent it corefers with and replaces part of:

   Show me a disk drive. No, a tape drive.

They can be produced as the other categories as well. So it is the
categorization based on reference and case frame match that primarily
determines the processing to be done.

3.1.3. Other factors in intended effects

Before we realized that coreference was the major factor in determining the intended effect of an antecedent elliptical utterance, we developed a table of intended effects based on the type of structural match, whether the antecedent was uttered by the same person or a different one, and whether it was marked as a question or not. This is presented here as table 3-1. Although this table ignores the reference relationship between the elliptical utterance and the antecedent, it is still interesting as an illustration of the information available from these sources. It is possible for several of the categories in a column of this table to be combined in a single ellipsis. When this happens, echoed parts merely help locate the match and have no influence on the intended effect, whereas replacements and extensions combine their effects in an additive fashion.

Antecedent phrase: *Give me a large disk.*

Type of ellipsis	Speaker	Intended effect
<Extension>?	Other	"Is this a correct guess?"
With dual ports?	Same	?"I'm unsure of this extension."
<Extension>*	Other	"I'm guessing this is right."
With dual ports.	Same	This elaborates the antecedent.
<Repetition>?	Other	"Is the echoed part correct?"
A large disk?	Same	?"I'm not sure this was correct."
<Repetition>*	Other	"This echo is what I heard."
A large disk.	Same	"This echo really is what I said." (Implies error on part of hearer.)
<Replacement>?	Other	"Is this what you actually meant?"
Tape drive?	Same	?"I may have actually meant this."
<Replacement>*	Other	"I'm assuming you meant this."
Tape drive.	Same	"I really meant this."

Table 3-1: Partial list of types of ellipsis/antecedent matches

The "*" indicates that the same punctuation as the antecedent utterance is used. This can lead to ambiguity, for example in the case where the antecedent utterance is a question. Also, when the antecedent utterance is an indirect question, "the same punctuation" can actually be a question mark, even though an explicit question mark was not used in the antecedent. Although punctuation is very unreliable in full sentences, where the syntax of the sentence provides additional information as to whether the utterance is a question, command, or statement, it is expected that in elliptical utterances users would be more exact in their punctuation, since there is no additional information available as to their intent. The utterances that are preceded with a "?" in the table are much less common, and less natural, than the others. Presumably this is because speakers rarely wish to question their own utterances.

3.1.4. Analysis of short story dialogues

In our initial investigation of ellipsis, we attempted to deduce a processing taxonomy by reading through all the short stories in the collection "Welcome to the Monkey House", by Kurt Vonnegut, Jr. [Vonnegut 70] Every instance of intersentential dialogue ellipsis that we found was recorded, assigned to a category of the evolving taxonomy, and re-assigned as the taxonomy changed. We also looked at a verbal protocol we had collected on an earlier project[4], to see if the types or frequencies of intersentential dialogue ellipsis there were markedly different.

The results of this investigation are presented in tables 3-2 and 3-3[5]. In these tables, "AR" stands for Antecedent (co)Referential, "AN" for Antecedent Non-coreferential, "CD" for Context Dependent, and "CF" for Context Free or Task Dependent.

From these results, it is apparent that referential antecedent ellipsis accounts for the majority of dialogue ellipsis, both in the short stories and in the actual dialogue. In the short stories, there are two instances where the majority of elliptical utterances were task-dependent, but both of these contained task-oriented dialogues, which are clearly special cases. Thus it is

---

[4]A natural language interface to a turbine blade factory shop scheduling system.

[5]Three of the twenty-five short stories contained essentially no dialogue, and therefore contained no dialogue ellipsis.

Overall in 630 literary examples:

AR	358	56.8 %
AN	30	4.8 %
CD	110	17.5 %
CF	132	21.0 %

Overall in 51 verbal protocol examples:

AR	37	73 %
AN	3	6 %
CD	11	21 %
CF	0	0 %

Table 3-2:   Statistics compiled on naturally occurring dialogue ellipsis

important for any system that understands elliptical utterances to handle the case of antecedent referential ellipsis.

While antecedent non-referential ellipsis accounts for only a small percentage of the ellipsis in these dialogues, command reformulation is widely believed to be an important use of ellipsis, and it is based on antecedent non-referential ellipsis. We believe this discrepancy is due to the master/slave nature of the typical man/machine interaction, versus the generally free-form interactions in these dialogues.

Context dependent ellipsis accounts for a significant percentage of ellipsis in both kinds of dialogues, but, as already pointed out, it is not directly relevant to linguistic processing, and can be quite difficult due to the wide scope of inferences possible. Similarly, context-free or task-dependent ellipsis seems to involve issues somewhat orthogonal to our concerns, although important for task-dependent man/machine interaction.

Story	AR#	AN#	CD#	CF#	Total#		AR%	AN%	CD%	CF%
1	8	0	1	2	11		73	0	9.1	18
2	18	3	3	2	26		69	11.5	11.5	7.7
3	10	2	4	5	21		48	9.5	19	24
4	18	3	16	5	42		43	7.1	38	12
5	24	5	12	4	45		53	11	27	8.9
6	20	2	3	1	26		77	7.7	12	3.8
7	11	0	6	19	36		31	0	17	53 *
8	13	0	6	3	22		59	0	27	14
9	4	1	6	22	33		12	3	18	67 **
10	24	0	4	3	31		77	0	13	9.7
11	16	0	1	0	17		94	0	5.9	0
12	24	0	2	11	37		65	0	5.4	30
13	4	0	2	0	6		67	0	33	0
14	23	0	4	5	32		72	0	12.5	16
15	12	0	5	3	20		60	0	25	15
16	27	0	10	14	51		53	0	20	27
17	31	3	3	5	42		74	7.1	7.1	12
18	4	0	0	1	5		80	0	0	20
19	32	4	6	4	46		70	8.7	13	8.7
20	6	0	6	1	13		46	0	46	7.7
21	18	2	10	13	43		42	4.7	23	30
22	11	5	0	9	25		44	20	0	36

* This contains a task-oriented dialogue: a chess game with spoken moves.
** Another task-oriented dialogue: a radio DJ reading dedications.

Table 3-3:   Literary ellipsis statistics broken down by short story

3.2. Other dialogue phenomena

The other dialogue phenomena that are treated by this system include noun phrase references and interactive error recovery.

3.2.1. Noun phrase references

Noun phrases are often treated by natural language systems as descriptions of sets of objects. The best current logical theories regard noun phrases as being sets of *sets* of objects. These two positions can be reconciled, by considering the noun phrase to be a set of sets, and the selection of a specific referent to be a selection of a specific set from the set of sets. Thus in this system there are *set descriptors*, which are abstract specifications of sets, and *concrete sets*, which are data structures describing sets consisting of specific objects. A set descriptor can be thought of as a set of sets, while the concrete set is a specific set from this set of sets that has been selected by a language- and context-dependent process.

Several kinds of noun phrases are understood by the current system. These were chosen to provide a non-trivial range of noun phrase references, and to allow an interesting variety of user interactions. There are clearly many other kinds of noun phrase components that could be added, including other kinds of quantifiers, and other special classes of adjectives, such as *next*. The implemented kinds of noun phrases are:

- **Definite**—A definite noun phrase, such as *the tape drive on the left*, is one that refers to a specific set of objects that the speaker expects the listener to be able to identify. Finding the referents of definite noun phrases in general is a very difficult unsolved problem, which has had much research devoted to it [Sidner 79, Grosz 77]. In this system, a very simple approach has been taken, which is to use the most recently mentioned set that matches the description. While this is known to be inadequate in general, it works well enough for our purposes here. There is no reason why the current approach could not be extended to be fully general, once a general computational solution to the problem is discovered.

- **Indefinite**—Indefinite noun phrases, such as *a dual ported disk drive*, are much easier to handle, since they specify any set that matches their description. This system handles such phrases by building set descriptors for them, and keeping track of which concrete sets eventually correspond to them, if such a relationship is later established. There are some additional complexities that the system does not handle, such as specific versus non-specific indefinites; in other words, whether there is a specific set that the speaker is thinking of, or whether any such set will do.

- **Generic**—Generics are noun phrases that refer to a type of object, as in *The disk drive is a mass storage device.* While handling generics is relatively simple, since there is only one data structure representing a given type, they can be quite difficult to identify. We are again taking a simple-minded approach, assuming that any definite reference for which we can find no specific referent is a generic.

- **Universally quantified**—This is any noun phrase with a quantifier like *all* or *every*. These correspond with the set of all sets containing all objects matching the noun phrase's description. There are again possible complicating factors, such as the use of a universal quantifier when one is actually thinking of a universe determined by the current context, but we again assume that for the moment we can ignore these difficulties.

- *Other*—Noun phrases such as *the other disk drive* or *another high density tape drive* are interesting because the word *other* and its relatives appear to indicate that the hearer is expected to identify some previously mentioned concrete set that is in the set of sets of objects that match this description, and then take a different, disjoint member of the set of sets that match the description as the referent. Since the referent should be disjoint from all such identifiable concrete sets, the hearer cannot simply take the first one found, but must identify all of them.

When an indefinitely described set is made concrete, for example when a specific set of objects is displayed in response to *Display some sternal ribs*, the system needs to record the objects' concrete set memberships, so that any later definite references will be able to tell which objects are being referred to. In addition, all old concrete sets must be available to the referent-finding routines, so that definite and *other* references can be resolved. Both of these considerations are implemented naturally in the context that a production system's working memory provides.

3.2.2. Interactive recovery from user errors

We have already seen in the taxonomy of ellipsis that a user can correct his or her own errors with an elliptical input, and we will see a detailed example of this in the next chapter. Here we wish to examine dialogue issues involved in interactive recovery from user errors.

In order to recover from an error, the system must first analyze the error, and decide what action is necessary. The fact that an error has occurred is often easily recognized, since the system fails to produce a complete interpretation for the input, but the type of error still requires some analysis[6]. The system currently detects some spelling errors, some grammar errors, reference errors, and, as a default, fatal errors. Only spelling errors and reference errors are corrected, spelling errors automatically and reference errors interactively.

A reference error is defined as a definite reference that cannot be a generic reference, and for which no referent has been found, for example *Show me the ribs* when no set of ribs is available. The reference error is detected at the end of the parse, when it is ascertained that the sentence as a whole does not have a verb phrase reference. A search is done back through the case frame structure until the original phrase lacking a referent is found. This will always be a noun phrase in the current system.

Two goals are then built, one to ask the user to identify the referent of this noun phrase, and the other to use the answer as the referent for the noun phrase. This initiates a recursive sub-dialogue, leaving the current parse in stasis in working memory while the same rules operate on the sub-dialogue. Doing this is easy because all the state of the system is in working memory, and can be ignored for a while and then resumed with no loss of information. Once the sub-dialogue is finished, the second goal causes the results to be incorporated into the original parse, and the original parse continues as if it had never been interrupted.

Natural language generation is done using the same case frame structures

---

[6]Some errors will cause the system to produce an erroneous interpretation, since the erroneous input appears to be a correct input, but different from what the user intended. Of course, such situations can be hard even for people to detect, unless the other speaker complains that the action taken was incorrect.

and the same general semantic chart representation as parsing, except that the system starts with a representation and produces natural language, rather than going in the other direction. This allows other processes that interact with natural language representations to work with a single type of representation, for example the error recovery rules above. More importantly, combined with the availability of objects in working memory, this allows the ellipsis resolution rules to deal with the previous utterance uniformly, whether it is an input or an output.

3.3. Relationship of theory to implementation

The next two chapters discuss the system as implemented. The relationship of the implementation to the theory underlying it is not direct. In other words, the taxonomy discussed in this chapter is not explicitly used in a decision tree by the program described in chapters 4 and 5, and the steps described here are not executed separately, as presented here. This is not to say that the theory presented in this chapter is totally divorced from the implementation. Rather, the theory is implicit in the design of the rules that carry out the ellipsis resolution. So the recognition of a potential elliptical fragment and the matching of its antecedent are both carried out by the built-in OPS5 matching process, since both are described in the left-hand side of the relevant rules. The instantiation of the resolved utterance is carried out by the right-hand side. The determination of intended effect is done by which rule fires, since different rules will fire for coreferent and non-coreferent utterances, and different types of structural match.

Thus the theory behind the implementation can be seen to a degree in the division of the processing into different rules, and in the structure of the rules, but not in the course of its processing. This is reasonable since a theory is an abstraction, whereas an implementation is a concrete object. There can be many useful theoretical descriptions of a single physical process, not all of which would be desirable as actual implementations.

We have implemented rules that understand subsets of each major class of antecedent ellipsis, with the exception of echo utterances, which do not appear to be very useful in a system using typewritten input. Further implementation of elliptical utterances for this domain would consist mainly of extending the syntactic coverage of the elliptical rules, and probably some minor redesign of mechanisms that prove not to be as flexible as intended, and would thus not be very interesting.

The implemented examples include a number of varieties of **reformulation** ellipsis (section 4.3, page 78), covering all four structural subcategories, and three varieties of coreferential ellipsis:

- a **correction** ellipsis (section 4.4.1, page 90)

- an **elaboration** ellipsis (section 4.4.2, page 91)

- a **question answer** (section 4.2.4, page 71)

The other dialogue phenomena discussed in this chapter have also been implemented.

As already mentioned, we did not implement non-antecedent ellipsis, since this seemed to primarily involve considerations outside the current project. We believe the whole taxonomy described is important for understanding ellipsis in general, and expect to eventually implement at least some examples of all the types, although perhaps in another system.

Chapter 4
The Implementation

In the previous chapter we discussed intersentential ellipsis and some other dialogue phenomena at a theoretical level, to understand in general how they should be treated by a natural language understanding system. In this chapter we will look in detail at the internal workings of a system based on the idea that an interactive dialogue is a single, continuous event rather than a series of separate transactions. This natural language interface is implemented in a production system using an extended chart parsing technique. The first example will be the interpretation of a relatively simple full-sentence input, to acquaint the reader with the basic operation of the system, followed by examples dealing with more challenging situations.

4.1. Top-level organization

The Psli3 production system cycles through four top-level phases:

Interpretation—In the interpretation phase, described in detail in section 4.2
below, the user is prompted for an input, and semantic
chart parsing is used to attempt to produce a single,
consistent interpretation of the user's utterance. Semantic
interpretation, ellipsis resolution, and reference resolution
are all carried out during the course of a "parse".

Installation—In the installation phase, backlink pointers are used to mark all
working memory elements that are part of the correct
interpretation.

Response—The response phase carries out whatever response is called for by
the user's utterance.

Garbage-collection—The garbage collection phase removes any unmarked
working memory elements from the previous parse, and
the cycle repeats.

4.2. Semantic chart parsing

We wanted to develop a parsing technique that would handle all kinds of
ambiguity in a simple, general fashion, without unreasonable inefficiency. It
also had to be adaptable to a production system architecture, so that
knowledge could be applied in an integrated and intuitively appealing
fashion. Starting with chart parsing [Kay 73] (explained cogently by
Winograd in [Winograd 83]) and modifying it to meet these goals lead to the
development of *semantic chart parsing*, so named to indicate the use of
semantic information in the chart and in the parser's rules.

In a syntactic chart parser, each grammar rule checks for the starting and
ending lexical positions of each constituent state it matches, and indicates the
starting and ending positions of the state it builds. In this way, partial
interpretations are indexed by the segment of the input they can account for.
A constituent is built only once on a given interval, and only those
constituents that are part of the interpretation of the whole input are seen in

the final result. In a *semantic* chart parser, such as the one in Psli3, a constituent can contain syntactic, semantic, and referential information, and is built only if its component parts are semantically and referentially, as well as syntactically, consistent. This is a natural extension when working in a production system, since everything in the system is done with rules, not just the syntax, and everything exists in states in working memory, not just the syntactic constituents. As noted in chapter 2, this method corresponds to a simple chart parser rather than an active chart parser. This is true both for the pragmatic reason that using the OPS5 rule matching mechanism prevents us from having access to partial matches of rules, and also the theoretical reason that active chart parsing only works for context-free rules, while OPS5 rules are Turing-equivalent. This too is natural, since the rules include the semantics of the natural language understanding system, which cannot, in general, be captured in context-free rules.

As was mentioned earlier, the production system language used for this system is OPS5 [Forgy 81]. In OPS5, all the rules are active at once. There is a single working memory, which consists of an unordered set of working memory elements, each of which has a class name and a fixed number of named slots. All rules that match the current contents of working memory are put into a *conflict set*. When more than one rule is in the conflict set, several general conflict resolution criteria are used to select one from the conflict set to fire. The programmer has a choice between two strategies: LEX and MEA. This system uses MEA, which simply means that the recency of the first element matched on the left hand side has priority over the recency of the other elements. This makes the system's conflict resolution behavior easier to control.

After the selected rule's actions are executed, this cycle repeats, allowing the other rules to fire if they still apply. In order to make this efficient for large numbers of rules and working memory elements, there is a caching discrimination network known as the RETE network. Only changes to the working memory are processed, and identical conditions shared by different rules are tested just once.

In our system, all of the procedural information is represented in terms of OPS5 production rules, except for Common Lisp input/output and database utility routines. When an operation is encoded by more than one rule, control flow between productions is handled by declarative *goals* in working memory. A goal is nothing more than a simple data structure describing an action that the system should carry out. Typically one rule will recognize what must be done and create a goal specifying an operation and any parameters to that operation, which are usually pointers to other objects currently in working memory. Other rules that match this goal then carry out the operation, followed by a rule that recognizes that the goal has been satisfied, and deletes it or marks it as fulfilled, if feedback is needed that the operation was successful. Although one can create complex goal structures in OPS5, most of the use of goals in this system is of this simple variety. For more information on OPS5 programming techniques, the work by Brownston et al. [Brownston 85] contains clear descriptions and many examples.

The information that would be encoded as grammar rules in a typical syntactic parser is encoded in our system in a more procedural form, in terms of OPS5 rules for lexicon access and for building case frame structure. However, because the lexicon has a very regular structure, the vast majority of lexical OPS5 rules are generated automatically on system start-up from declarative lexicon entries in the semantic network[7]. A typical lexicon production rule and its English translation are shown in figure 4-1, and the corresponding declarative lexicon entry is shown in figure 4-2. Each lexicon entry can give rise to several production rules, in this case two, one for declarative and one for imperative verb phrases[8].

This parser operates in a left-to-right, primarily bottom-up, breadth-first fashion, generating all the interpretations that it is going to generate in parallel. Since chart parsing is basically a data structure organization technique, the control aspects of the parser are independently determined in its design. One could build a semantic chart parser that proceeded in a right-to-left, depth-first, top-down order. Left-to-right interpretation was chosen to make the design of the system's rules easier, since events occur in roughly the order they do in human parsing. If this system were connected to a speech understanding system rather than typed input, an island-driven

---

[7]Nouns, verbs, and case markers are generated from the semantic network entries. Function words and interjections such as **goodbye** are defined by hand-crafted lexicon rules. Names of people are handled by a rule that accesses semantic network information. Punctuation is handled by a rule that accesses a list of internal punctuation markers created by the input function.

[8]Questions in general are not currently handled. They could probably be handled using special rules that refer to the declarative lexicon entries.

```
(p dict-show-imp
   (input ^word << show name present give >> ^utt nil ^utt nil
          ^state <s> ^position <pos> ^prev <prev> ^next <next>)
   (state ^state <s> ^status posted ^utt <n>)
  -->
   (bind <new-state> (gint))
   (make state ^state <new-state> ^status posted ^utt <n>)
   (make ancestor ^state <new-state> ^ancestor <s>)
   (bind <name> (gint))
   (make pos ^utt nil ^type verb ^con <name> ^state <new-state>)
   (make pos ^utt nil ^type verb-phrase ^con <name> ^tense nil
             ^state <new-state> ^status 1)
   (make act-reference ^action display ^mode imp ^token <name>
                       ^e-subj t ^state <new-state>)
   (bind <e2> (gint))
   (make expect ^type e-marked ^con <name> ^marker for ^state
         <new-state> ^token <e2> ^slot bene ^required nil)
   (bind <e3> (gint))
   (make expect ^type e-unmarked ^con <name> ^marker 2nd ^state
         <new-state> ^token <e3> ^slot object ^required t)
   (bind <e4> (gint))
   (make expect ^type e-marked ^con <name> ^marker to ^state
         <new-state> ^token <e4> ^slot recip ^required nil)
   (bind <e5> (gint))
   (make expect ^type e-unmarked ^con <name> ^marker 1st ^state
         <new-state> ^token <e5> ^slot recip ^required nil)
   (make word-seq ^first <pos> ^last <pos> ^prev <prev>
                  ^next <next> ^state <new-state>))
```

RULE dict-show-imp:
IF   there is an input word that is one of: show, name, present, give
       and it is in a posted state for utterance n
THEN   obtain a unique name for a new state
       make a new posted state indicator for utterance n
       make a backlink to the input word
       obtain another unique name
       indicate that this state is a verb part-of-speech
       indicate that it is also a verb phrase part-of-speech
           with one required case
       indicate that it is an imperative display action with no subject
       obtain four more unique names
       indicate an expectation for a "benefactor" marked by "for"
       indicate an expectation for an "object" as a direct object
       indicate an expectation for a "recipient" marked by "to"
           or as an indirect object.
       indicate the segment of the input that it represents
           (this is last for consistent conflict resolution)

Figure 4-1:   Production rule defining imperative *show*

approach might be preferred. A primarily breadth-first, bottom-up approach
was chosen for the following reasons:

```
(dict-show (is-a verb)
           (referent display)
           (word show name present give)
           (past showed named presented gave)
           (required-case actor object)
           (expect (subj actor)
                   (for bene)
                   (2nd object)
                   (to recip)
                   (1st recip)))
```

Figure 4-2:   Sample lexicon frame from semantic network

- Since the system should notice true ambiguities in the user's input, it needs to generate all viable alternatives. Breadth-first generation is the most straightforward way of doing this. The system is not totally breadth-first, however, since interpretations that are less plausible, i.e., those which involve error-correction actions, are only generated if there are no likelier interpretations. This is a very weak form of best-first search. If other highly reliable pruning criteria were available, the system could be made to operate in true best-first fashion.

- Sentence fragments (ellipsis) and erroneous input require bottom-up capabilities, since the system cannot predict, top-down, all possible errors, and cannot constrain the allowable types of fragments to any great degree. In a system dealing with more complex syntactic constructions, more top-down control could be added.

- The use of a largely breadth-first, bottom-up approach does not present major difficulties in terms of efficiency due to the use of a chart and semantics within the parsing process. As we will see, the chart structure avoids the replication of common low-level structures within different high-level structures that would occur in a simple breadth-first, bottom-up approach. The early use of semantics prevents structures from being placed into the chart in the first place if they do not make sense at least locally.

There is also some psychological justification for this approach. Experiments on eye fixation in reading [Carpenter 81] have found that for a number of milliseconds all common meanings for the word just read are available. The unused readings rapidly fade from memory, even before the whole sentence has been read. While strong expectations can bias the reader in terms of how strongly some readings are activated, the others are still present. While this system is not a detailed psychological model, it is our belief that natural language systems that at least roughly follow human practices will have the greatest chance for long-term success.

4.2.1. An example parse

Our extended chart parsing approach will be explained by example, using the sentence

> *Show me xn* [sic] *irregular bone*

This sentence contains three types of local ambiguity. The most noticeable is that there is a spelling mistake, where *xn* could be corrected to be either *an* or *in* using the current lexicon and spelling corrector (a Common Lisp version of [Durham 83]). The second local ambiguity is the case relationship of *me* to *show*. In this sentence, *me* is the recipient of the action, whereas in

> *Show me to your friends*

it is the object being shown. Thus in a left-to-right parse, the case of *me* is locally ambiguous. The third local ambiguity is whether the word *bone* is part of the idiomatic phrase *irregular bone* or refers to the general *bone* concept. The system currently does not handle adjectives; when a frame in the database has a multiple word name, it is treated as an idiomatic phrase, where the individual words carry no meaning, but the phrase as a whole refers to the frame. In the current application, a medical database, there is a frame called irregular_bone, which represents the set of all irregularly-shaped bones.

Figure 4-3 shows the chart built during the parse of this sentence[9]. Each line segment in the diagram represents a state built by one or more OPS5 production rules, usually defining a newly found constituent of the sentence. These constituent states can contain syntactic, semantic, and referential information, and generally represent either case frame structures or semantic structures such as sets of semantic network frames. The vertical axis is time, starting at the top and finishing at the bottom; the horizontal axis is the

---

[9]This diagram was produced by an actual run of the system, using a few tracing productions. One of these fires whenever a new state is created and the goal of tracing is active, and prints a line of relevant information on the terminal.

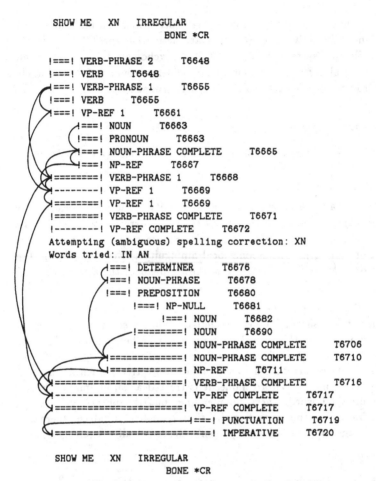

```
SHOW ME   XN    IRREGULAR
                    BONE *CR


!===! VERB-PHRASE 2      T6648
!===! VERB      T6648
!===! VERB-PHRASE 1      T6655
!===! VERB      T6655
!===! VP-REF 1       T6661
   !===! NOUN        T6663
   !===! PRONOUN        T6663
   !===! NOUN-PHRASE COMPLETE       T6665
   !===! NP-REF       T6667
!========! VERB-PHRASE 1       T6668
!--------! VP-REF 1       T6669
!========! VP-REF 1       T6669
!========! VERB-PHRASE COMPLETE       T6671
!--------! VP-REF COMPLETE       T6672
Attempting (ambiguous) spelling correction: XN
Words tried: IN AN
         !===! DETERMINER       T6676
         !===! NOUN-PHRASE        T6678
         !===! PREPOSITION        T6680
            !===! NP-NULL       T6681
               !===! NOUN       T6682
         !========! NOUN       T6690
         !========! NOUN-PHRASE COMPLETE       T6706
!==============! NOUN-PHRASE COMPLETE       T6710
!==============! NP-REF       T6711
!======================! VERB-PHRASE COMPLETE       T6716
!----------------------! VP-REF COMPLETE       T6717
!======================! VP-REF COMPLETE       T6717
                    !===! PUNCTUATION       T6719
!============================! IMPERATIVE       T6720


    SHOW ME    XN    IRREGULAR
                BONE *CR
```

Figure 4-3: Chart built for *Show me xn* [sic] *irregular bone*

location of the segment in the input. For clarity, the only backlinks shown
are those for states that are part of the correct interpretation. The actual
representation used for a state is shown in figure 4-4, along with an English
translation. This representation consists of a set of working memory
elements, each containing the unique name of the state in its "state" field.

Once the goal for parsing is activated, a production fires that prints a
prompt, and then takes the user's input words and puts them into a list of
working memory elements, linked by their numerical positions in the input.

```
(STATE ^STATUS POSTED ^UTT 1 ^STATE T6655)
(ANCESTOR ^ANCESTOR I6645 ^STATE T6655)
(POS ^CON T6656 ^TYPE VERB ^STATE T6655)
(POS ^CON T6656 ^STATUS 1 ^TYPE VERB-PHRASE ^STATE T6655)
(WORD-SEQ ^FIRST 1 ^LAST 1 ^NEXT 2 ^PREV 0 ^STATE T6655)
(ACT-REFERENCE ^TOKEN T6656 ^ACTION DISPLAY ^MODE IMP ^E-SUBJ T
                ^STATE T6655)
(EXPECT ^TOKEN T6660 ^CON T6656 ^TYPE E-UNMARKED ^MARKER 1ST
                ^SLOT RECIP ^STATE T6655)
(EXPECT ^TOKEN T6659 ^CON T6656 ^TYPE E-MARKED ^MARKER TO
                ^SLOT RECIP ^STATE T6655)
(EXPECT ^TOKEN T6658 ^CON T6656 ^TYPE E-UNMARKED ^MARKER 2ND
                ^SLOT OBJECT ^REQUIRED T ^STATE T6655)
(EXPECT ^TOKEN T6657 ^CON T6656 ^TYPE E-MARKED ^MARKER FOR
                ^SLOT BENE ^STATE T6655)
```

State t6655 has been posted (it is active), as part of utterance 1.
This state is backlinked to state i6645 (an input word).
This state represents a verb part-of-speech.
This state also represents a verb phrase, with 1 required case.
This state represents the first word of the input.
This state contains action t6656, which is a "display" action, in imperative
    mood, with the subject already taken care of.
This state expects an indirect object for action t6656, which will be the
    recipient of the action,
or a recipient contained in a prepositional phrase marked by "to".
This state expects a direct object for action t6656, which will be the
    object acted on by the action, and is a required case.
This state expects a prepositional phrase marked by "for", which will be the
    benefactor (who the action is done for).

Figure 4-4: Actual representation of state t6655 in working memory

The leftmost and rightmost words of the utterance are marked, as are the
leftmost and rightmost words of each "sentence"[10] within the utterance.
This much is done by a Common Lisp function call within this production.
The production also creates a data structure indicating that this is an action
taken by the speaker. Several rules fire that manipulate system goals,
turning the parser on, and then the first parsing rule fires, activating the
left-most word of the input. In order to ensure left-to-right parsing, a
working memory element representing an input word must be activated
before any of the parsing productions can act on it. The next word is only
activated when no more rules can fire on the current word.

---

[10]"Sentence" here means a sentence or elliptical utterance separated from others by a period,
question mark, exclamation point, or end of input.

Interpretation of this input begins as the first two lexicon rules fire, placing two interpretations of *show* into working memory, one for the declarative mood (state T6648 in figure 4-3) and one for the imperative (T6655). The second interpretation, shown in detail in figure 4-4, indicates that it is an imperative display action, a verb and a verb phrase, and that it spans the interval [1:1]. Several expectations are also placed into this state, indicating which syntactic markers correspond to which cases of this verb, as an imperative.

Now the rule that creates an initial referent for imperative verbs fires, building a proposed action of displaying, with none of its cases filled (T6661). The approach to verb phrase reference taken in this system is that an imperative refers to a hypothetical action. If the hearer carries out the request, the hypothetical action becomes a real action, namely the one the hearer has just performed. For a declarative verb phrase, a referent would have to be searched for among actions the system already knew about. As is the case for all states, the interval of the input this state covers and the ancestor state that is its constituent are recorded.

At this point, all the rules that can fire on the input seen so far have fired, so a pair of rules fires that activates the next word. There is a pair of rules because one sometimes wants to ensure that a rule fires after all regular rules have fired, to do error-detection, for example. So the first rule creates a goal that indicates that all regular parsing rules have fired on the active part of the input, and, after allowing any pending rules to fire, the second rule deletes this goal and activates the next word of the input. The rule for *me* now fires, indicating that the word located on the interval [2:2] is a noun referring to the special token *me*, and that it is a pronoun (T6663). A rule then fires that takes a noun that is not preceded by any prenominal parts of a noun phrase, such as quantifiers or determiners, and builds a new noun phrase containing it (T6665). This is marked as a "complete" noun phrase, because its head noun has been found.

This rule makes use of a special mechanism to prevent multiple firings, since otherwise it could fire more than once, because any number of states that are "not a determiner" could exist in the preceding position. The mechanism is simply to create a "bindings" working memory element that indicates the rule's name, its lexical starting and end position, and any significant variable bindings. The rule tests for the existence of such an element before firing, so that it will only fire once for each location and set of bindings[11]. Now the rule that finds a referent for *me* fires, in response to the special *me* token. All it currently does is to indicate (T6667) that the referent is the current speaker. In a more complete system this would take into account other situations, for instance when *me* is in a quotation of someone else speaking.

The first of two verb phrases on the interval [1:2] is now started (T6668), by a rule that fills the first unmarked case, or indirect object, of a verb phrase with an adjacent noun phrase. This makes *me* fill the deep recipient of *show*, and creates a "constraint" element that says that the recipient case is filled. The existence of this state as a descendant of another verb phrase (the single word *show*), with a non-required case filled, causes a simple "demon"[12] rule to fire that indicates that this verb phrase has the same number of unfilled required cases as its ancestor. Another rule then fires that takes the referent of the ancestor verb phrase, the referent of the noun phrase, and the case relationship established between them syntactically, and produces a referent for the new verb phrase, which is simply the display action with a recipient of the speaker (T6669). State T6669 is "proposed" rather than "posted", which means that some other rule must approve it before other parser rules can act on it. In figure 4-3, this situation is represented by a single dotted line rather than a double one. Proposed states allow separate semantics checking rules to prevent semantically impossible referents from being built. Another demon fires, indicating that, since the recipient case was filled in the ancestor verb phrase, it is filled in the current verb phrase. This constraint propagation is done by copying "constraint" elements between states. Finally, one of the semantics rules associated with the display action fires, indicating that the speaker is indeed a semantically acceptable recipient for the display action.

The construction of the other verb phrase on [1:2] (T6671) proceeds along similar lines, with two differences. The first is that the case filled this time

---

[11]This corresponds to a problem in syntactic chart parsers, when using them for ATNs and other non-context-free parsers. Some method for including the context in the chart's index must be used. Currently the rules that start noun phrases, look up database names, attach prepositional phrases to noun phrases, and resolve ellipsis use this mechanism.

[12]In OPS5 production systems, a demon is simply a rule that pays no attention to goals, but carries out some simple computation or consistency check that is always needed when a particular situation arises.

is the direct object, which can also be referred to as the second unmarked object, as in the lexicon frame in figure 4-2. This is a required case for *show*, so a demon fires that indicates that there is one less unfilled required case. Since this leaves no unfilled required cases, a second demon fires, indicating that this verb phrase is now syntactically "complete". The second difference with this case is that for *show*, the direct object corresponds to the deep object case, and *me* is not acceptable to the semantic rules as an object of *show*. So the referent for this interpretation of the first two words (T6672) remains proposed, and never becomes posted.

No more rules can fire on the input activated so far, so once again the two input-advancing rules fire. This activates the misspelling *xn*, which does not trigger any rules. So the first input-advancing rule fires again, creating a goal that says all parsing rules have fired. This, combined with the lack of any descendants from the input word *xn*, causes the rule that spots unusable words to fire, creating a goal of fixing an error in a word[13]. The spelling-correction rule then fires, marks the input *xn* as having been checked for spelling errors, and calls a Common Lisp routine that places all possible respellings it can find into working memory as new input elements, on the same interval. This causes input elements for *an* and *in* to be placed in working memory, both on [3:3], just as the original input was. These incompatible interpretations coexist in the chart without any problem, and are both available to any rules looking for words on this interval.

The lexicon rule for *an* now fires, indicating that it is an indefinite determiner (T6676). This causes a rule to fire that takes a determiner that is not preceded by a quantifier and starts a new noun phrase on [3:3] with it (T6678). The noun phrase in this case is not marked complete because there is not yet any head noun in it. The lexicon rule for *in* fires, indicating that it is a preposition (T6680). The two rules then fire again that advance the input.

The new word is *irregular*, which is the beginning of the idiomatic phrase *irregular bone*. A rule fires that indicates that this is a known word with a null interpretation (T6681). This is done so that error-correction rules will not spuriously fire on an unused initial word of an idiom. The input-

---

[13]Truly novel words are handled correctly by this mechanism. See section 4.2.4 for the details.

advancing rules fire again, bringing *bone* into activation, and the lexicon rule for a bare *bone* fires, indicating that it is a singular noun on [5:5] referring to the bone frame (T6682), and loading the bone frame into working memory from the semantic network. This is done by creating a goal to load the frame, which is then executed by another rule, using a Common Lisp function[14], if the frame is not already present in working memory. This prevents multiple copies of a frame from appearing in working memory. The bone frame is shown in figure 4-5 as it appears in the semantic network, and in figure 4-6 as it appears after being loaded into working memory as a set of "fact" elements. Although the state representing a lone *bone* is built, it will not be used by any other rules, since there are no compatible adjacent states.

```
(bone (is-a anatomical_thing)
      (located-in human_body)
      (instances flat_bone irregular_bone
                 long_bone short_bone))
```

Figure 4-5:   Bone frame in semantic network

```
(FACT ^ID T9229 ^SCHEMA BONE ^SLOT IS-A ^FILLER ANATOMICAL_THING)
(FACT ^ID T9230 ^SCHEMA BONE ^SLOT LOCATED-IN ^FILLER HUMAN_BODY)
(FACT ^ID T9231 ^SCHEMA BONE ^SLOT INSTANCES ^FILLER FLAT_BONE)
(FACT ^ID T9232 ^SCHEMA BONE ^SLOT INSTANCES
                            ^FILLER IRREGULAR_BONE)
(FACT ^ID T9233 ^SCHEMA BONE ^SLOT INSTANCES ^FILLER LONG_BONE)
(FACT ^ID T9234 ^SCHEMA BONE ^SLOT INSTANCES ^FILLER SHORT_BONE)
```

Figure 4-6:   Bone frame in working memory

At this point, the presence of the input word *irregular* and the following word *bone* allow the lexicon rule for *irregular bone* to fire, indicating that it is a singular noun on [4:5] referring to the frame irregular_bone (T6690). This rule also loads the frame representing irregular_bone into working memory. The possible presence of the word *in* on [3:3] allows the new noun phrase rule to fire, creating a noun phrase on [4:5] consisting of just this frame (T6706). A rule then fires that takes the noun phrase started by *an* at [3:3] and extends it to include *irregular bone*, producing a syntactically complete, indefinitely determined noun phrase (T6710) on [3:5]. This allows a referent-building rule to fire, creating a set descriptor on [3:5] for a singleton set of things that are irregular bones (T6711).

---

[14]This Common Lisp function is descended from one in a FranzLisp SRL/OPS5 interface built by Brad Allen.

The existence of the complete noun phrase on [3:5], along with the verb phrase on [1:2], allows the rule that fills direct object cases of verb phrases to fire again, creating a verb phrase (T6716) on [1:5]. The rule checks to make sure the case it is filling is not filled yet in the verb phrase, by making sure there is no constraint element for it[15]. This check prevents the other verb phrase on [1:2] from being used to build another verb phrase on [1:5]. Thus an incorrect local interpretation can exist in the chart without interfering with other, correct interpretations. Once again, the new verb phrase is marked as complete, and a new action with this set as its object is proposed (T6717). This time, however, there are two "constraint" elements propagated into the new state, one for the recipient case and one for the object case; also, the semantic rule associated with objects of display actions fires, indicating that the proposed action is semantically acceptable, so a posted verb phrase reference now exists on [1:5].

No more parsing rules can fire, so the input-advancing rules again fire. This brings the last input element into activation. A lexicon rule fires, indicating (T6719) that there is an end-of-sentence punctuation at [6:6][16]. Finally, because there is a verb phrase with a known referent extending from the beginning of the utterance to an end-of-sentence punctuation mark, a rule fires that builds a request for the described action (T6720), and indicates that it is an imperative sentence spanning the whole utterance [1:6].

The rule that notices that there are no other rules to fire now acts, but, since this is the end of a "sentence", the rule that fires next does not advance the input, but indicates that we are at the end of a sentence. Since there is a state spanning the whole utterance, a correct, consistent interpretation has been found, so a rule fires indicating parsing success and terminating the parsing phase. In the installation phase, the "ancestor" elements of states that are part of the correct interpretation are traced back in order to capture the completed parse, and their states are marked as being part of this utterance. The states not included in the correct parse are eventually deleted from working memory, when the garbage collection phase occurs.

---

[15]The constraint elements are necessary because the syntax of OPS5 rules makes it impossible to otherwise test for the case not being present.

[16]A blank line containing only a carriage return is currently regarded as an end-of-sentence punctuation mark.

4.2.2. Current syntactic coverage

Now that the overall behavior of the system has been described, the current range of covered phenomena will be examined, as summarized in table 4-1. As was mentioned on page 54, the "expectations" used in this system to handle verb phrase syntax are loaded into working memory when a lexical entry for a verb is loaded, and indicate the correspondence between surface syntactic cases and deep verb cases for that verb. There are four rules for adding cases to a verb phrase, one each for the subject, indirect object, direct object, and one for all marked cases.

Clause moods	Clause surface cases	Nominal surface cases
imperative	subject	quantifier
declarative	direct object	determiner
wh-questions	indirect object	*other*
	marked cases	marked cases

Table 4-1: Syntactic coverage

The rule for the second object, or direct object, is shown in figures 4-7 and 4-8. It matches an expectation for a direct object, a verb phrase (clausal) case frame with a filled subject[17] and the corresponding deep case free, and a noun phrase adjacent to the verb phrase. It then produces a new state, representing the clausal case frame with the noun phrase filling the direct object slot and the corresponding deep case. Figure 4-9 shows a schematic diagram of the case frame structure built to represent the input in the example, *Show me an irregular bone*. Terms beginning with capitals, such as Act-reference or Display, are case frames or constants, respectively. Terms in all capitals are names of objects known to the system, such as the login name of a user it knows. Terms in lower case are slot names. Terms such as "t6656" are unique identifiers used to establish references between structures. For example, "Reference t6686" refers to "t6712" in its "deref:" slot, which is the set of irregular bones described by "Schema-spec t6712"[18]. The nesting of structures is implemented as pointers, so there is no actual

---

[17]In our system, imperatives are represented as verb case frames whose subjects are already filled when loaded into working memory.

[18]These identifiers are usually numerically close to the corresponding state's identifier, but never exactly the same, since the state is a different entity from the object built within the state.

difference in the data structure between the "object:" slot of Act-reference
t6656 being filled with Reference t6686, and the "deref:" slot of Reference
t6686 being filled with Schema-spec t6712. The diagram is drawn so that the
first case frame structure is the representation for the utterance and the
second case frame structure represents the referent of the utterance.

```
(p e-unmarked-2nd
    (expect ^type e-unmarked ^con <cname> ^marker << 2nd obj >>
                ^token <etok> ^state <older1> ^slot <slot>)
    (POS ^type verb-phrase ^con <cname> ^state <bigger1>
        ^utt nil)
    (state ^state <bigger1> ^status posted ^utt <n>)
    (word-seq ^utt nil ^first <vpf> ^prev <vpp>
                ^last <vpl> ^next <npf> ^state <bigger1>)
    { (act-reference ^token <cname> ^e-subj <> nil
                        ^state <bigger1>)                    <act> }
;;; This is necessary since you can't say "^<slot>" in OPS5:
    - (constraint ^slot <slot> ^type case ^state <bigger1>)
    (word-seq ^utt nil ^first <npf> ^last <npl> ^next <npn>
                ^state <older3>)
    (state ^state <older3> ^status posted ^utt <n>)
    (POS ^utt nil ^type noun-phrase ^status complete
        ^con <npname> ^state <older3>)
    -->
    (bind <new-state> (gint))
    (make state ^utt <n> ^state <new-state> ^status posted)
    (make POS ^utt nil ^type verb-phrase ^con <cname>
        ^state <new-state>)
    (make ancestor ^state <new-state> ^ancestor <bigger1>)
    (make ancestor ^state <new-state> ^ancestor <older3>)
    (make act-reference ^1 (substr <act> 1 inf) ^<slot> <npname>
                    ^e-2nd t ^state <new-state>)
    (make constraint ^element <cname> ^slot <slot> ^type case
                    ^filler <npname> ^state <new-state>)
    (make word-seq ^first <vpf> ^last <npl> ^prev <vpp>
                    ^next <npn> ^state <new-state>))
```

Figure 4-7:   Production rule defining direct object

The rule for the indirect object differs from the direct object rule mainly in
that it checks the partially-built verb phrase to make certain that there is
not already[19] a direct object in the clausal case frame. The rule for the
subject makes certain that no nominal cases have been added to the verb

---

[19]Since case frames are built up from the input in a left-to-right direction, the indirect object
rule can be phrased in terms of which cases are currently present when this noun phrase is
encountered, allowing a fairly simple and natural description.

RULE e-unmarked-2nd:
IF   there is an expectation for an unmarked 2nd object for
        concept <cname> corresponding to slot <slot>
      and there is a verb phrase representing <cname> in state <bigger1>
      and state <bigger1> is posted as part of utterance <n>
      and this state starts at <vpf> and goes to <vpl>,
        preceded by <vpp> and followed by <npf>
      and the act-reference describing <cname> already has a subject
      and slot <slot> has not yet been filled in this state
      and there is a state <older3> going from <npf> to <npl>,
        followed by position <npn>
      and state <older3> is posted in utterance <n>
      and this state represents a complete noun phrase <npname>
THEN   obtain a unique name for a new state
      make a new posted state indicator for utterance n
      indicate that it is a verb phrase part-of-speech
        representing <cname>
      make a backlink to the verb phrase's state
      make a backlink to the noun phrase's state
      make this act-reference just like the previous one, except
        slot <slot> gets <npname>, and 2nd object is filled
      indicate separately that <slot> is filled by <npname>
      indicate that this state goes from <vpf> to <npl>, after <vpp>
        and before <npn>

Figure 4-8:   English version of rule defining direct object

phrase yet, and also has the position of the noun phrase before the verb
phrase, since the surface subject occurs before the verb in English. The rule
for marked cases includes a match of a preposition, and requires that the
preposition be the same as the one that the expectation indicates is the
marker of the case.

The imperative and declarative forms of a verb are handled by loading two
separate sets of expectations, generated from the same semantic network
frame, where the imperative has no expectation for a surface subject, and its
surface subject is indicated as already being filled in its initial clausal case
frame. Interjections and pragmatic utterances, such as *goodbye,* are treated
as imperatives without expectations or referents, and are understood to be
implicit requests. The other sentential form that is currently handled is the
wh-subject question, such as

    Which ribs are false ribs?

This is treated syntactically as a declarative sentence, using the declarative
form of the verb. Other forms of wh-questions are not handled, since they
involve additional syntactic phenomena such as AUX inversion. This is a

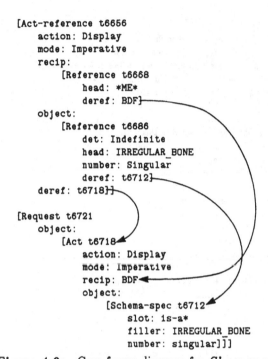

```
[Act-reference t6656
    action: Display
    mode: Imperative
    recip:
        [Reference t6668
            head: *ME*
            deref: BDF]
    object:
        [Reference t6686
            det: Indefinite
            head: IRREGULAR_BONE
            number: Singular
            deref: t6712]
    deref: t6718]]

[Request t6721
    object:
        [Act t6718
            action: Display
            mode: Imperative
            recip: BDF
            object:
                [Schema-spec t6712
                    slot: is-a*
                    filler: IRREGULAR_BONE
                    number: singular]]]
```

Figure 4-9:   Case frame diagram for *Show me an irregular bone*

limitation of the system as implemented, not a general limitation of the method[20].

The semantic checking of clausal case fillers mentioned previously is handled by parameter-checking rules associated with the action described, which mark the proposed state as posted if the noun phrase's referent is acceptable as the indicated parameter. The current rules check for the referent being either animate or present in the semantic network, depending on the case in question, but could be of arbitrary complexity, involving numerous rule firings.

Noun phrases in the current system allow for quantifiers, determiners, the special adjective *other*, a head noun, and prepositional phrases. For each

---

[20]We have in previous versions of this system implemented other, more difficult, syntactic phenomena, such as non-subject relative clauses. Our handling of such phenomena uses derived categories, as in GPSG.

category except quantifiers and prepositional phrases, there are two rules: one to attach the constituent to a previously-started noun phrase to its left, and one to start a new noun phrase with this constituent as its leftmost element. *Another* has a special rule, since it fills both the determiner and the "other" cases, and always starts a new noun phrase. Previous versions of the system included relative clauses and conjunctions, but without the noun phrase reference capabilities described in section 4.2.3 below.

For each category, the rule that starts a new noun phrase requires that there be at least one state to its immediate left that is not an incomplete noun phrase. This prevents new noun phrases from being hypothesized where they cannot be correct. It then creates the new noun phrase, and sets the deep case representing this constituent to an appropriate value, either one of a fixed set of values (for quantifiers, determiners, and "other") or the name of a semantic network frame for a noun. The rule that adds the current category to a previously-started noun phrase simply matches the noun phrase and the new word, and makes sure that the corresponding case is not yet filled in the noun phrase. Then it creates a new noun phrase including the new word, with the deep case filled appropriately.

The description above deals solely with the sentence-local, non-referential side of noun phrase processing, since noun phrase reference is covered below. Prepositional phrase attachment, however, combines the two processes, so that the syntactic creation of a noun phrase—prepositional phrase link depends on the referential acceptability of the semantic specification thus created. This is implemented by having the rule for attachment propose both a syntactic/semantic and a referential representation state, and then checking with the semantic network as to whether this attachment is a reasonable possibility[21]. If it is, another rule changes both states to being posted rather than proposed.

4.2.3. Verb and noun phrase reference

Our approach to imperative verb phrase reference has already been described. Although the system can handle declarative sentence syntax, it does not currently handle declarative verb phrase references, since they are

---

[21]Since the semantic network in question only stores extensional information, this amounts to a check as to whether such a referent exists.

not needed in the database retrieval domain. To add them to the system, a referent search similar to the one described below for noun phrases would be needed, to search for past event descriptions, in addition to other additions to the system's semantic capabilities. The other type of sentence is the question. Wh-subject questions look like declarative sentences, except that the subject is a wh-noun phrase, and the sentence ends in a question mark. These features are recognized by the rule that builds a wh-subject question reference, which simply builds a representation of the state described and indicates that its mood is interrogative[22].

Rule	Quant	Determ	Number	Set descriptor created
Indef1	none	indef	singular	new set, type X, singular
Indef2	none	indef	plural	new set, type X, plural
Indef3	none	none	plural	new set, type X, plural
Universal	univ	either	either	new set, type X, univ, plural
Generic1	none	def	singular	new set, prototype X, singular
Generic2	none	none	either	new set, prototype X, singular
Qnp	none	wh-word	either	new set, identity of subordinate set
Definite	none	def	either	pointer to referent set

Table 4-2:   Coverage of noun phrase reference

The current referent-finding rules for personal pronouns and names are trivial. The coverage of other types of noun phrase reference is summarized in table 4-2. As discussed in chapter 3, a noun phrase can be described as a set of sets of objects, and its referent as being a set of objects selected from this set of sets. The process of finding the referent of a noun phrase corresponds to making this selection. In discussing how different noun phrases refer to sets in different ways, we are discussing how this selection is made. The two main kinds of noun phrase references are definite and indefinite. Definite references, such as *the ribs*, refer to some uniquely

---

[22]The state so constructed is actually just a representation of the meaning of the question, rather than a true reference. It can be thought of as a decision that there is no referent.

identifiable set of objects, although not always one explicitly mentioned in
the dialogue, whereas indefinite references, such as *a rib*, refer to any set
matching their description; the selection is arbitrary as far as language use is
concerned. From here on, we will describe sets simply as data structures,
rather than as set-theoretic sets. A rigorous set-theoretic treatment of noun
phrases and their referents, along the lines indicated in chapter 3, is possible,
but it is a difficult task somewhat orthogonal to this work.

Indefinite references are relatively simple to implement, since they do not
involve search. There are three rules in this system for generating simple
indefinite referents. The one matches unquantified, singular, indefinitely
determined noun phrases, while the other two match unquantified, plural,
and either indefinitely determined or non-determined noun phrases[23]. In
either case, a set descriptor is built that describes a set of objects of the type
indicated by the head noun, and of either singular or plural number,
respectively[24]. Then a new copy of the nominative reference is created,
which has this set as its referent. The selection of a specific concrete set for
this to correspond to is done arbitrarily by the display rules, when they need
to make a decision to display a specific object.

Universally quantified references are handled by a similar rule, since again
no search is required. The set descriptor created indicates a set of objects of
the type of the head noun, with universal quantification and plural number,
even for surface-singular phrases such as *each rib*. Generic references,
which are references to classes rather than individuals, as in

   The rib is a long bone

require another simple rule, matching singular, unquantified, definitely
determined noun phrases for which the search for a referent has failed. The
set descriptor indicates the singleton set consisting of the object representing
the head noun, rather than a set of objects of its type. There is also a rule
for another type of generic, which is discussed in section 4.2.4. References for
wh-noun phrases, those that have *which* or *what* as a determiner, are
created by building a set descriptor for a frame called *identity*, whose object

---

[23]The rule for non-determined plurals is activated during reference error repair, discussed in
section 4.2.4.

[24]A "plural" set descriptor indicates that the set it matches may have more than one element,
whereas a "singular" set descriptor is constrained to match a set with only one element.

slot is filled with a normal set descriptor for the rest of the noun phrase. This indicates that the wh-noun phrase represents, in our system, the identity of the modified noun phrase.

As mentioned above, definite references require a search for a previous referent. When there are no modifiers, this is simply a search for a set of the correct type, as in the third sentence here:

> *Show me a rib.*
> **RIB_NUMBER_11**
> *Show me a long bone.*
> **FEMUR**
> *Show Bill the rib.*
> **RIB_NUMBER_11**

The referent search for a definite noun phrase with no modifiers is started by a rule that creates a goal of doing a "type-search" with a set descriptor indicating a set of objects of the type indicated by the head noun. Three rules implement the search to find all sets of objects in working memory of the type indicated by the set descriptor. The first creates, for each immediate instance[25] of the type, a "fact" working memory element indicating that the instance *is-a** the type. *Is-a** indicates the transitive closure of the "is-a" relationship, and is a pseudo-slot, in that no slot by that name exists in the semantic network. The first rule also loads the frame, if it is not already present in working memory. The next rule implements the transitivity of *is-a**, so that if type 2 *is-a** type 1, and has an instance of type 3, it creates a new fact that says type 3 *is-a** type 1. The third rule simply creates the goal of loading any frame that has an *is-a** fact, but no real frame slots loaded. There are also several bookkeeping rules, which make sure that all *is-a** facts for a given slot have consistent set memberships and display status information. As soon as a fact exists that indicates that a previously created set *is-a** the type of the current noun phrase, the definite reference rule fires, deleting the goal for type-searching and indicating that the current noun phrase refers back to the earlier set[26]. Since this set has already been elaborated into specific objects that were displayed, the use of a definite reference will in general have a different effect than the use of a similar indefinite one.

---

[25]*Instance* is, in this system, the inverse of *is-a*.

[26]This may occur before any rules act on the type-search goal.

Locative prepositional phrases, as in

Display an irregular bone in the face

are the only type of modifier currently implemented. The representation for such a modified noun phrase's set descriptor involves an additional pseudo-slot called *in**, which is the transitive closure of the "contains", "has-part", and "is-a" relationships. The *in** slot in the modified noun phrase's set descriptor is filled by the set descriptor for the modifying noun phrase. This is illustrated by figure 4-10. The existence of the specified set is verified before the parser will create the phrase, by a "location-search" similar to the type-search discussed above, with a parallel set of three rules. These rules search down the contains and has-part links, while the type-search rules, which are also activated by the location-search goal, do any searching down is-a links that may be necessary.

When a definite reference includes a modifier, the referent must be a previous set that matches the full current description:

Display an irregular bone in the face.
PALATE
Display another irregular bone.
SPHENOID
Show Bill the irregular bone in the face.
PALATE

The referent search for a definite noun phrase with such a modifier starts as before. However, since the system has already located the referent in verifying the permissibility of the prepositional phrase attachment, the rule always succeeds immediately. An additional demon rule indicates that phrases of the form *the flat bones in the face* should be regarded as having the first noun phrase universally quantified.

The only remaining aspect of the system's noun phrase reference to be discussed is the interpretation of terms like *other*. This works basically like definite reference, except that the reference is to a set that this set must be disjoint from, rather than equal to, and is a separate, parallel constraint on the set created by the rules above. There are two rules that recognize that an "other" situation has occurred, one for wh-noun phrase references and one for regular references. Each of these creates a type-search goal and indicates that the system is looking for "other" sets, by creating an empty *other-than* slot in the reference's set descriptor. There is another rule, which matches an already existing set that fits the noun phrase's description, and indicates that

```
[Act-reference t1942
    action: Display
    mode: Imperative
    object:
        [Reference t1951
            det: Indefinite
            head: IRREGULAR_BONE
            number: Singular
            deref: t1996
            modifiers: T]
                [Reference t1987
                    det: Definite
                    head: FACE
                    number: Singular
                    deref: t1993
                    modifyee: t1951
                    modification: Location]
        deref: t2073]

[Request t2076
    object:
        [Act t2073
            action: Display
            mode: Imperative
            object:
                [Schema-spec t1996
                    slot: is-a*
                    filler: IRREGULAR_BONE
                    number: Singular]
                [Schema-spec t1996
                    slot: in*
                    filler:
                        [Schema-spec t1993
                            schema: FACE
                            number: Singular]]]]
```

Figure 4-10:   Case frame diagram for:
Display an irregular bone in the face

this set's elements must be disjoint from the new set's elements, by adding to the new set's descriptor an *other-than* slot filled with a pointer to the set. It also turns off the type-search goal. This goal may be reactivated, however. When a user says, for example,

> *Show me all the other ribs*

if there have been several sets of ribs displayed, the new set must be disjoint from all the preceding ones. So there is a rule that turns the type-search goal back on again if there are more old set descriptors around, and the search has not been exhausted yet. Finally, another rule acts when a noun phrase contains an "other" slot, but the search fails to find any previous set descriptors that match the noun phrase's description. This rule creates an "other-than" set descriptor with a filler of *none, which is treated as an error flag during the response phase.

4.2.4. Error recognition and recovery

As was indicated on page 56 in section 4.2.1, the system is able to recognize and correct certain classes of errors, using a set of rules that are each tailored to a particular type of error. There are currently two modes of error-correction: word error repair and high-level error repair. A word error repair goal is created when all normal rules have fired on a word that can and the word has no descendant states, i.e., nothing recognized it. Two rules exist for fixing this type of error. The first attempts to spelling correct the word, as previously described. The second takes a failed spelling correction attempt and indicates that the unknown word should be treated as an uninterpreted string, possibly a new frame's name[27]. In previous versions of this system, database names not in the lexicon were also recognized in this error-repair phase, but the current system handles this situation with a production that fires during normal processing, when a lexicon rule would.

A high-level error repair goal is created when the system is at the end of a sentence, all normal rules have fired, and there is no single state spanning the whole input. This signifies that the system was unable to interpret the input as a coherent unit. Three general types of high-level errors are currently recognized: syntax errors, reference errors, and fatal errors. The fatal error rule fires if no other high-level error rules can fire, and just prints out an apology, creates a dummy state covering the whole input[28], and moves on to the next sentence. This can be caused by inputs such as

Would you be so kind as to display something?

which contains several words and constructions the system does not understand. Some syntax errors, as in

Show display a rib

are recognized by a rule that fires if there is a pair of contiguous states that

---

[27]This makes it impossible in the current system for a new word to be recognized as such if it is the same as an old word, or can be spelling corrected to one.

[28]This indicates to the system that it has dealt with the input.

together cover the whole input except the punctuation, as shown in figure
4-11. The punctuation is not included because purely syntactic states in this
system do not include final punctuation. The goal created by this rule is
handled at the moment by a single rule, which simply prints out a message
saying where the break occurred, builds a dummy state, and moves on to the
next sentence.

```
        SHOW DISPLAY
                A     RIB   *CR

!===! VERB-PHRASE 2      T2363
!===! VERB        T2363
!===! VERB-PHRASE 1      T2370
!===! VERB        T2370
!===! VP-REF 1          T2376
      !===! VERB-PHRASE 2        T2378
      !===! VERB        T2378
      !===! VERB-PHRASE 1        T2384
      !===! VERB        T2384
      !===! VP-REF 1          T2389
            !===! DETERMINER      T2391
            !===! NOUN-PHRASE        T2393
                  !===! NOUN        T2395
            !========! NOUN-PHRASE COMPLETE      T2401
            !========! NP-REF      T2402
      !============! VERB-PHRASE COMPLETE        T2404
      !--------------! VP-REF COMPLETE      T2405
      !============! VP-REF COMPLETE        T2405
                  !===! PUNCTUATION      T2407
```

  Sorry but there seems to be a syntax error around word 2

Figure 4-11:   Chart built for *Show display a rib*

Reference errors occur when a definite noun phrase has no referent. For
example, if a user says

Show me the ribs

when no plural set of ribs exists in the current discussion[29]. Such a situation
and its resolution are shown in figures 4-12 and 4-13. A reference error goal
is created if there is a single state that spans the entire sentence up to the
final punctuation that does not have a referent, such as state T0121 in figure

---

[29]The system could assume in this case that the user meant **all the ribs**, but it does not
currently make this assumption unless there is a locative modifier in the noun phrase.

4-12. This indicates that the sentence produced an internally consistent interpretation, but some non-local reference in it did not succeed. This goal causes a search through the backlinks of the state in question for the constituent that caused the problem. The search uses a set of six rules. The first rule creates a goal for each ancestor of the top state, to check it for a reference problem. Another rule creates a goal for the situation where there is a top-level noun phrase that must be checked. The search proceeds in a breadth-first fashion. For each ancestor, one of four cases applies:

- The state cannot have a reference—this is a state that represents something like a preposition. The goal for this state is deleted.

- The state has a reference—the goal is again just deleted.

- The state is a verb phrase with no reference—this causes the search to move down to this branch, and begin again, recursively.

- The state is a noun phrase with no reference—this is the source of the problem (state T0076 in figure 4-12).

There are three rules that can fire here. If the noun phrase is a bare, singular noun, such as in *Show me irregular_bone*, a rule fires that makes a generic reference for it, and deletes both the local goal and the reference error goal[30]. Similarly, a bare, plural noun, as in *Show me flat bones*, causes an indefinite plural reference to be constructed. The other rule asks the user for a better identification. It deletes the local goal, builds the internal representation of a question consisting of the problem noun phrase with the new determiner *which*, and creates goals to generate an input error question and use the answer to fix a reference error. The goal to generate an error-repair question causes a rule to fire that updates the count of utterances, creates a goal turning on natural language generation, and builds an internal representation of the fact that the system is taking an action in response to the user's action of speaking (state T0133). The system then activates its natural language generator, described in detail in section 4.2.5, below.

---

[30]This rule acts during error repair for two reasons: this construction seems intuitively to require an extra cognitive effort, and in the case of an elliptical noun phrase a bare noun may have an elided quantifier or determiner. If this rule acted during normal parsing, one would get an ambiguous reference where one should not occur.

```
+ show me the ribs

SHOW ME    THE  RIBS *CR

!===! VERB-PHRASE 2      T0040
!===! VERB      T0040
!===! VERB-PHRASE 1      T0047
!===! VERB      T0047
!===! VP-REF 1       T0053
     !===! NOUN      T0055
     !===! PRONOUN      T0055
     !===! NOUN-PHRASE COMPLETE      T0057
     !===! NP-REF      T0059
!========! VERB-PHRASE 1      T0060
!--------! VP-REF 1      T0061
!========! VP-REF 1      T0061
!========! VERB-PHRASE COMPLETE      T0063
!--------! VP-REF COMPLETE      T0064
        !===! DETERMINER      T0066
        !===! NOUN-PHRASE      T0068
           !===! NOUN      T0070
        !========! NOUN-PHRASE COMPLETE      T0076
!==================! VERB-PHRASE COMPLETE      T0121
              !===! PUNCTUATION      T0122


!============================! RESPONSE      T0133
!============================! DIALOGUE-SEG      T0134


           !=============! QUESTION      T0135
               !===! PUNCTUATION      T0137
           !========! NOUN-PHRASE      T0136
           !===! HEAD      T0140
        !===! DETERMINER      T0139
        !===! WHICH      T0142
           !===! RIBS      T0141
              !===! ?      T0138
WHICH RIBS ?
```

Figure 4-12:   Chart built during reference error repair (first half)

After the natural language output has been generated, another error-repair rule removes the goal of natural language generation, and sets up the goal structure for parsing the answer. The system then parses the answer in its usual fashion. If the user's input is a lone noun phrase, a special question-answer ellipsis rule fires, which simply makes a "statement" out of the noun phrase, for the final special question-answer rule to handle. After the assembly of the parse is finished, this final rule takes the referent of the

```
+ any ribs

                                      ANY  RIBS *CR

                                      !===! DETERMINER      T0154
                                      !===! NOUN-PHRASE     T0156
                                        !===! NOUN          T0158
                                      !========! NOUN-PHRASE
                                               COMPLETE     T0160
                                      !========! NP-REF      T0161
                                             !===! PUNCTUATION
                                                            T0163
                                      !=============! ELLIPSIS
                                                            T0164
Ready to assemble a meaning for state T0164

                        !==================! RESPONSE     T0167
!========================================! DIALOGUE-SEG      T0168

        !========! NP-REF      T0166
!------------------! VP-REF COMPLETE     T0169
!=================! VP-REF COMPLETE     T0169
!======================! IMPERATIVE     T0171
Ready to assemble a meaning for state T0171
```

Figure 4-13: Chart built during reference error repair (conclusion)

elliptical answer and makes it the referent of the questioned noun phrase[31]
(state T0166). It also creates a representation indicating that the answer was
a response to the question (T0167), and deletes the goals that were involved
in the user interaction. The resulting interaction appears thus:

> *Show me the ribs.*
> **WHICH RIBS?**
> *Any ribs.*
> <Ribs displayed>

The noun phrase in the original input now has a referent. This allows the
parse to proceed, generating referents for the other states, which are still
sitting in working memory from the original parse attempt. The parse
succeeds and is then responded to in the normal fashion.

---

[31]This should actually be a more involved process, which would check to make sure the new
referent really could fit the old noun phrase.

4.2.5. Natural language generation

As was mentioned in chapter 3, on page 42, the natural language generator was designed to be as similar to the parser as possible, so that all natural language utterances would have the same type of internal representation. This means that it must generate a semantic chart representing an utterance as it generates the utterance.

The natural language generator starts with a simple internal representation of the utterance the system intends to generate. It then:

- Elaborates the specification—it adds the necessary information to turn this representation into a chart state

- Generates the output tree—it produces chart states representing the intermediate-level constituents of the output and the literal output words

- Determines chart positions—it marks the leaves of the tree with their position in the output, and then uses these positions to produce absolute beginning and ending points for states representing higher level constituents

- Optionally displays its chart—if the parser is tracing its actions, the generator's chart is displayed next, as in the chart at the bottom of figure 4-12

- Prints output—the output is printed on the screen left to right

- Garbage collects—finally, any goals left over from the trace's tree walk are deleted.

The first step of this process is started by a rule that matches a natural language generation goal that has a question as its specification. It adds state, part-of-speech, backlink, and positional markers to the question and its noun phrase, based on information already present in the specification, and adds a state indicating that the utterance ends with a question mark. Similar rules for various parts of speech generate a "parse tree" representing the output, including the actual lexical items to be printed, which are stored as "output" working memory elements. The case frame representation of the utterance generated in figure 4-12 is shown in figure 4-14. The lexical items for nouns[32] that are in the lexicon are built by rules that are created automatically at system start-up time from the semantic network lexicon entry, just like the corresponding parsing rules. Figure 4-15 shows a typical lexicon entry, the one for the domain-dependent idiomatic term *irregular bone*. Figure 4-16 shows the corresponding rule that the system builds during start-up. There is also a rule for generating the lexical items for database entries that are not in the lexicon.

```
[Question t0127
   object:
      [Reference t0128
         det: Which
         head: RIB
         number: Plural]]
```

Figure 4-14: Case frame diagram for *Which ribs?*

```
(dict-irregular_bone (is-a noun)
         (referent irregular_bone)
         (double-s (irregular bone))
         (double-p (irregular bones)))
```

Figure 4-15: Sample nominal lexicon frame

In the design of the generator, a problem that arose immediately was that positional information in the parser's chart is represented in terms of absolute positions in the input utterance. Absolute positions are not available for states built in the early phases of generation, since one does not generally know how long the utterance is going to be until one has produced the full tree and can count the leaves. The solution is to record during generation the states that precede and follow the state being generated, and then link them together via a tree walk once all the leaves have been generated.

There are three rules that determine the order of leaf nodes. The first simply tells a leaf with no predecessor state that it is first. The second takes a state that knows its absolute position, and a leaf that has the state as its predecessor, and indicates that the leaf is in the next absolute position. This correctly handles all cases except that of a multiple word lexical item, which has no tree structure between its individual words. In this case the trailing words are handled by the third rule. Four back-propagation rules tell the

---

[32]The generator currently only has rules for generating noun phrases. Lexical generation rules for verbs could also be created automatically.

```
(p print-dict-irregular_bone-2-s
    (goal ^name nlg ^status active ^spec <n>)
    (pos ^utt <n> ^type head ^object irregular_bone
          ^number << nil singular >> ^state <n-state>)
    (word-seq ^state <n-state> ^utt <n> ^first <a> ^last <b>
              ^next <c> ^prev <d>)
  - (ancestor ^ancestor <n-state>)
  -->
    (bind <new-state> (gint))
    (bind <new-state2> (gint))
    (make ancestor ^state <new-state> ^ancestor <n-state>
          ^utt <n>)
    (make output ^word irregular ^position nil ^prev <d> ^next
          <new-state2> ^utt <n> ^state <new-state>)
    (make ancestor ^state <new-state2> ^ancestor <n-state>
          ^utt <n>)
    (make output ^word bone ^position nil ^prev <new-state>
          ^next <c> ^utt <n> ^state <new-state2>))
```

RULE print-dict-irregular_ bone-2-s

IF   there is an active nlg goal for utterance <n>
      and utterance <n> has a singular irregular_ bone NP head <n-state>
      and its state goes from <a> to <b>, preceded by <d>
          and followed by <c>
      and it has no descendant states yet
THEN   obtain a unique name for a new state
      obtain another unique name for another state
      indicate that the new state's ancestor is <n-state>
      make an output element for the word "irregular", preceded by <d>
          and followed by the other new state
      indicate that the other new state's ancestor is <n-state>
      make an output element for the word "bone", preceded by the first new state
          and followed by <c>

Figure 4-16: Production rule for generating *irregular bone*

ancestor states what their absolute locations are. They simply tell states that
have the same predecessor or successor as one with a known starting or
ending position, respectively, that they have the same absolute endpoint.
These rules work in an interleaved fashion with the leaf ordering rules to
mark the whole tree.

Since the chart display for generation, if called for, must happen after the
actual generation of the chart, special care must be taken to produce a
display that is sensible. This is done by using goals that walk down the tree,
the goals for the children of a state only being created once the parent state
has been displayed. Five rules handle this: two to manipulate goals, one to
display interior states, and two to display leaf states, which ensure that the

leaves are displayed left-to-right by storing the current position in the top-level goal's specification field.

The actual output of the utterance is carried out by two rules, one to print out the first word, and one to print out the rest, using a mechanism similar to the one used by the chart display above. A single rule deletes any goals remaining from tracing the generator's chart.

4.3. Ellipsis handling in the chart

In chapter 3, we saw that antecedent elliptical utterances could be divided into four categories on the basis of the type of processing they require:

- **Reformulation**—This is a non-coreferential utterance, where ellipsis is used simply to take advantage of shared structure between otherwise unrelated utterances.

- **Correction**—A coreferential utterance where there is replacement of case frame structure in the antecedent implies that the user is correcting the previous utterance.

- **Elaboration**—A coreferential utterance where there is only additional case frame structure added to the antecedent is an elaboration of the antecedent.

- **Echo**—Where there is a simple repetition of a piece of the antecedent, the utterance is an echo, generally to verify that the piece in question was communicated correctly.

There was also a separate, structural description of the elliptical utterance itself, in terms of what part of the utterance was elided:

- **Clausal Functional**—The verb phrase (clausal) case frame was elided, leaving one or more pieces of substructure with no superstructure.

- **Clausal Constituent**—Constituents of the clausal case frame were elided, leaving a verb phrase with missing parts.

- **Nominal Functional**—The noun phrase (nominal) case frame

was elided, leaving one or more pieces of its substructure
orphaned.

- **Nominal Constituent**—Constituents of the nominal case frame
  were elided, leaving a noun phrase with missing parts.

While this division is less important at a general level, the actual production
rules that resolve elliptical utterances are also partitioned along these lines,
since they match constituent pieces of the case frames involved.

For reformulation elliptical utterances, which are the most typical variety
in database retrieval, examples of both functional and constituent ellipsis for
both clausal and nominal case frames are handled. In the following two
subsections, the details of reformulation ellipsis resolution will be described.
In section 4.4 below, examples of correction and elaboration ellipsis resolution
will be presented. As mentioned earlier, no examples of echo ellipsis
resolution were implemented.

The main use of the chart in the examples in the current section is in
handling ambiguity. The various proposed resolved case frames can be
placed into working memory in parallel positions, and the ones that do not
succeed will not in any way interfere with the correct interpretation. Section
4.4 makes a more interesting use of the special properties of the semantic
chart technique.

4.3.1. Verb phrase reformulation ellipsis

To begin with another example, suppose that the following sequence
occurred:

> *Show me an irregular bone*
> **THORACIC_ VERTEBRA**
> *Some flat bones*

The chart produced by the system in interpreting this reformulation ellipsis
is shown in figure 4-17. This noun phrase is parsed in the same way as the
noun phrase in the previous example, until the indefinite noun phrase
reference in state T1764 is produced. At this point we have a noun phrase at
the left end of an utterance, which causes the rule shown in figures 4-18 and
4-19 to fire. This is the rule for unmarked verb phrase functional ellipsis at

the beginning of an input. As such, it must find a previous verb phrase[33], and create a new verb phrase in which this noun phrase replaces a case in the previous verb phrase. The case may be either marked or unmarked in the antecedent sentence, but must be filled; potential cases that are not filled in the antecedent sentence must be explicitly marked by a preposition in the ellipsis.

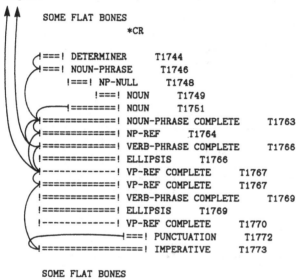

```
         SOME FLAT BONES
                      *CR

      ===! DETERMINER      T1744
      ===! NOUN-PHRASE       T1746
         !===! NP-NULL        T1748
            !===! NOUN        T1749
               !=======! NOUN        T1751
      =============! NOUN-PHRASE COMPLETE      T1763
      =============! NP-REF      T1764
      =============! VERB-PHRASE COMPLETE      T1766
      !============! ELLIPSIS       T1766
      -------------! VP-REF COMPLETE      T1767
      =============! VP-REF COMPLETE      T1767
      !============! VERB-PHRASE COMPLETE      T1769
      !============! ELLIPSIS       T1769
      !------------! VP-REF COMPLETE      T1770
               ------------!===! PUNCTUATION      T1772
      =================! IMPERATIVE       T1773


         SOME FLAT BONES
                     *CR
```

Figure 4-17:   Chart built for *Some flat bones*

This rule fires twice in this example. The first time (T1766), it replaces the object of the antecedent, to produce the equivalent of

> *Show me some flat bones*

Then a rule fires that continues verb phrase references from antecedent verb phrases to elliptical verb phrases, in the same way that verb phrase references are continued within single sentences. This proposed verb phrase reference (T1767) then gets approved by the same semantic rule that approved the original filler of the object case. The case frame structure for the antecedent is shown in figure 4-20, and for the resolved ellipsis in figure

---

[33]Because of the recency criterion used in determining which instantiations of OPS5 rules are allowed to fire, the most recent utterance satisfying the rule's left-hand side will always be selected.

```
(p ellipsis-initial-1-unmarked
    (input ^utt nil ^utt nil ^position <npf> ^end left)
    (word-seq ^utt nil ^first <npf> ^last <npl> ^prev <npp>
                ^next <npn> ^state <older3>)
    (state ^state <older3> ^status posted ^utt <n>)
    (POS ^utt nil ^type noun-phrase ^status complete
        ^con <npname> ^state <older3>)
    (reference ^token <npname> ^deref nil ^state <older3>)

    (expect ^con <cname> ^token <etok> ^state <older1>
            ^slot <slot>)
    ( << request question >> ^utt { <n0> <=> 0 } ^object <acttok>
                            ^state <rstate>)
    { (act-reference ^token <cname> ^deref <acttok>
                    ^utt { <n0> <=> 0 })              <actref> }
    (constraint ^element <cname> ^slot <slot> ^type case)
    - (constraint ^slot <> <slot> ^type case ^state <older3>)
    - (goal ^name cp-understand-error-answer ^status subgoaled)
    - (bindings ^rule ellipsis-initial-1-unmarked ^first <npf>
                ^last <npl> ^bindings <older3> <rstate> <slot>)
    - (bindings ^rule ellipsis-initial-1-unmarked ^first <npf>
                ^last <npl> ^bindings <unbound1> <unbound2>
                                        <unbound3> { <> <n0> } )
    -->
;;; Build a new state.
    (bind <new-state> (gint))
;;; The state is posted, since it doesn't need semantic checking:
    (make state ^utt <n> ^state <new-state> ^status posted)

;;; This is built for display purposes
    (make POS ^utt nil ^type ellipsis ^con <cname>
            ^state <new-state>)
    (make POS ^type verb-phrase ^con <cname> ^status complete
            ^state <new-state> ^utt nil)
    (make ancestor ^state <new-state> ^ancestor <rstate>)
    (make ancestor ^state <new-state> ^ancestor <older3>)
;;; Inhibit further rule firings using same expectation.
    (make bindings ^rule ellipsis-initial-1-unmarked ^first <npf>
            ^last <npl> ^bindings <older3> <rstate> <slot> <n0>)
;;; Propose the connections.  Inhibit expectations.
;;; Also makes this part of a new concept, and a new utterance.
    (make act-reference ^1 (substr <actref> 1 inf) ^utt nil
            ^deref nil ^<slot> <npname> ^state <new-state>)
    (make constraint ^element <cname> ^slot <slot> ^type case
                    ^filler <npname> ^state <new-state>)
    (make word-seq ^first <npf> ^last <npl> ^prev <npp>
                ^next <npn> ^state <new-state>))
```

Figure 4-18: Production rule for unmarked, initial, verb phrase
functional ellipsis

RULE ellipsis-initial-1-unmarked:
IF   the left end of the input sentence is <npf>
        and state <older3> goes from <npf> to <npl>, preceded by <npp>
            and followed by <npf>
        and this state is part of utterance <n>
        and this state is a complete noun phrase named <npname>
        and this state does not have a referent assigned
        and verb phrase <cname> has a case named <slot>
        and previous utterance <n0> was a request for or question about
            act <acttok> in state <rstate>
        and verb phrase <cname> was used to refer to <acttok>
        and the case named <slot> was filled in the previous utterance
        and this noun phrase is not assigned to some other slot
        and we are not in a question answering situation
        and this rule has not fired on this location for this noun phrase,
            sentence, and slot yet
        and this rule has not fired on this location for an earlier utterance
THEN   obtain a unique name for a new state
        build a posted state for utterance <n>
        indicate that this state is an ellipsis
        indicate that this state is a verb phrase
        indicate that this state has ancestor <rstate>
        indicate that this state has ancestor <older3>
        indicate that this rule has now fired on this location, noun phrase,
            sentence, slot, and utterance
        build a copy of verb phrase <cname> with <slot> now filled by
            <npname> as part of the new state and current utterance
        indicate a constraint that case <slot> is filled by <npname>
            in the new verb phrase
        indicate that this state covers the same interval as <npname>

Figure 4-19:   English version of rule for unmarked, initial, verb phrase
functional ellipsis

4-21. Notice that the Act-reference in figure 4-21 has the same identifiers for
itself[34] (T1661) and the recipient (T1671) as the Act-reference in the
antecedent.

The second time (T1769), the ellipsis rule replaces the recipient of the
antecedent, to produce the equivalent of
    Show some flat bones an irregular bone
This in turn produces a proposed verb phrase reference (T1770), which fails

---

[34]That is, its unique identifier is the same identifier as in the antecedent, indicating that it is a
copy of that case frame.

```
[Act-reference t1661
    action: Display
    mode: Imperative
    recip:
        [Reference t1671
            head: *ME*
            deref: BDF]
    object:
        [Reference t1682
            det: Indefinite
            head: IRREGULAR_BONE
            number: Singular
            deref: t1710]
    deref: t1713]]

[Request t1716
    object:
        [Act t1713
            action: Display
            mode: Imperative
            actor: *PSLI*
            recip: BDF
            object:
                [Schema-spec t1710
                    slot: is-a*
                    filler: IRREGULAR_BONE
                    number: singular]]]
```

Figure 4-20:   Case frame diagram for antecedent:
Show me an irregular bone

to get approved by the semantic rules for the display action. These case
frame structures are shown in figure 4-22. There is no Request because the
verb phrase reference failed to get approved. These are the only two ellipsis
resolutions created, even if there are other previous sentences in working
memory, due to the bindings mechanism described on page 55. This
mechanism is used twice in the left-hand side of each initial ellipsis rule, once
to prevent multiple firings as described earlier, and a second time just
matching the utterance number, so that only the most recent utterance that
can be the antecedent will be used. At this point, the two rules that advance
input fire, and then the rule that recognizes punctuation fires. The rule for
recognizing a request then fires, just as before, since the resolved elliptical
phrase now appears to be a verb phrase from the beginning of the input up
to a punctuation mark.

The rule for an initial marked case, such as

```
[Act-reference t1661
    action: Display
    mode: Imperative
    recip: t1671
    object:
        [Reference t1747
            det: Indefinite
            head: FLAT_BONE
            number: Plural
            deref: t1765]
    deref: t1768]

[Request t1774
    object:
        [Act t1768
            action: Display
            mode: Imperative
            actor: *PSLI*
            recip: BDF
            object:
                [Schema-spec t1765
                    slot: is-a*
                    filler: FLAT_BONE
                    number: plural]]]
```

Figure 4-21:   Case frame diagram for resolved ellipsis:
(Show me) Some flat bones

To Bill

is similar to the rule for an initial unmarked case, except that it matches an input that starts with a preposition, requires that the case be a marked case for the antecedent's verb, and does not require this case to have been filled in the antecedent. There is also a rule for extending an initial ellipsis by adding a marked case to it, as must happen for the second noun phrase in

Some flat bones to Bill

or

To Bill for me

This is similar to the rule for extending a normal verb phrase by adding a marked case to it, except that it does not require the head verb to be in the current sentence.

There is also a rule for a second unmarked noun phrase in an ellipsis, such as

Show me an irregular bone
Bill some flat bones

```
[Act-reference t1661
    action: Display
    mode: Imperative
    recip:
        [Reference t1747
            det: Indefinite
            head: FLAT_BONE
            number: Plural
            deref: t1765]
    object: t1682
    deref: t1771]

[Act t1771
    action: Display
    mode: Imperative
    actor: *PSLI*
    recip:
        [Schema-spec t1765
            slot: is-a*
            filler: FLAT_BONE
            number: plural]
    object: t1710]]
```

Figure 4-22:   Case frame diagram for incorrectly resolved ellipsis:
(Show) Some flat bones (an irregular bone)

This situation must be handled by a special case rule, since there can only be two unmarked cases, and they must be the indirect object and direct object of the antecedent verb. Presumably this constraint is related somehow to the fine details of how English-speakers parse indirect objects.

While handling multiple, non-contiguous fragments like these is easy and natural in a case frame based system with bottom-up capabilities such as this one, network based approaches, such as ATNs and semantic grammars, cannot cope with them at all unless they step outside their normal parsing paradigm [Hayes 86, Carbonell 83]. These approaches do not generally have access to information about individual cases, which are the natural unit in ellipsis. Also, they are inherently top-down, and have great difficulties separating the different constituents, which are easily found using bottom-up techniques.

In a system that understood declarative sentences[35], the ellipsis rules for

---

[35]As mentioned in section 4.2.3, the system handles declarative syntax, but not declarative references.

initial ellipses could cause some concern, since they would fire every time there was a subject, or a leading prepositional phrase, in a declarative sentence. There are two possible solutions for this. The current approach is to simply let it happen, since the spurious ellipsis resolution just goes into the chart, and will not affect anything global as long as the sentence does indeed have a verb in it. A more sophisticated approach would be to rewrite the rules so that the ellipsis rules would only fire once the whole utterance had been scanned, and no consistent interpretation had been found for it.

The other major form of verb phrase ellipsis, constituent ellipsis, occurs in sentences such as

> *Show me an irregular bone*
> *Show Mark*

where a required case is omitted. There is a single rule that handles this situation, by producing a new verb phrase on the same interval, with the missing case filled from the corresponding case in the antecedent sentence. This is shown in case frame form in figure 4-23, assuming that the antecedent is the sentence in figure 4-20. Only required cases are filled in this way, because otherwise almost every sentence would be considered elliptical, since there would be some optional cases not expressed. It is our belief that such resolution should only be done where the semantics of the system really requires it, and then by a non-linguistic inference process.

```
[Act-reference t1751
    action: Display
    mode: Imperative
    recip:
        [Reference t1761
            head: MSF
            deref: MSF]
    object: t1682
    deref: t1771]]

[Request t1773
    object:
        [Act t1771
            action: Display
            mode: Imperative
            recip: MSF
            object: t1710]]
```

Figure 4-23:   Case frame diagram for resolved ellipsis:
Show Mark (an irregular bone)

An antecedent sentence for an ellipsis may be a previously resolved ellipsis. For example, in the sequence

Show Fred a long bone
A short bone
Show Bill

the final ellipsis must be resolved as *Show Bill a short bone*, using the resolved second ellipsis as its antecedent. This is not a problem, as long as the writer of the ellipsis rules has been careful to write them in such a fashion that they refer to deep representations, such as the instantiated case frames, and not surface ones when looking for an antecedent. These sentences are handled correctly in our system.

The other main ellipsis dialogue situation handled in the current system is an elliptical answer to a question. The mechanism for generating a question and parsing an answer was covered in detail in subsections 4.2.4 and 4.2.5. There is a separate rule for handling the case where a noun phrase appears as the answer to a wh-question. This is because in this case, the context of having a wh-question posed creates a strong expectation that a noun phrase uttered in response will fill the gapped case indicated by the wh-word, so the more general case productions must be overridden by one that specifically takes the noun phrase as the answer to the question. In a hypothetical variation of the previous example:

Show me the ribs.
    Show you which ribs?
Any ribs.

the usual verb phrase ellipsis rule would try to substitute *any ribs* for each of the noun phrases in the antecedent, whereas the question-answer ellipsis rule will override, and only substitute *any ribs* for the wh-phrase *which ribs*.

4.3.2. Noun phrase ellipsis resolution

As with verb phrases, there are two kinds of noun phrase ellipsis. Currently the only form of functional noun phrase ellipsis handled is a lone, locative prepositional phrase, such as

Show me some flat bones.
In the face.

This is handled by a rule similar to the one that does normal prepositional phrase attachment, except that it looks in a previous utterance for the noun phrase to attach to. This produces a new noun phrase on the same interval as the isolated prepositional phrase, which is then available to the verb phrase ellipsis rules as a functional ellipsis to be resolved. This is shown in case frame diagrams 4-24 and 4-25.

```
[Act-reference t1555
    action: Display
    mode: Imperative
    recip:
        [Reference t1566
            head: *ME*
            deref: BDF]
    object:
        [Reference t1577
            det: Indefinite
            head: FLAT_BONE
            number: Plural
            deref: t1601]
    deref: t1604]]

[Request t1607
    object:
        [Act t1604
            action: Display
            mode: Imperative
            actor: *PSLI*
            recip: BDF
            object:
                [Schema-spec t1601
                    slot: is-a*
                    filler: FLAT_BONE
                    number: Plural]]]
```

Figure 4-24: Case frame diagram for antecedent:
Show me some flat bones

The form of constituent noun phrase ellipsis currently handled is a lone noun phrase that has no quantifier or determiner, as in the pair

> *Show me a true rib.*
> *False rib.*

In this situation, the missing quantifier and determiner come from the old noun phrase that is replaced by the new noun phrase during verb phrase ellipsis resolution. The rule that handles this matches a lone noun phrase without a quantifier or a determiner, its resolved verb phrase, and the corresponding noun phrase in the antecedent sentence. It then produces a new noun phrase, with the quantifier and determiner from the antecedent

```
[Act-reference t1556
    action: Display
    mode: Imperative
    recip: t1566
    object:
        [Reference t1577
            det: Indefinite
            head: FLAT_BONE
            number: Plural
            deref: t1665
            modifiers: T]
                [Reference t1653
                    det: Definite
                    head: FACE
                    number: Singular
                    deref: t1659
                    modifyee: t1577
                    modification: Location]
    deref: t1669]

[Request t1702
    object:
        [Act t1669
            action: Display
            mode: Imperative
            actor: *PSLI*
            recip: BDF
            object:
                [Schema-spec t1665
                    slot: is-a*
                    filler: FLAT_BONE
                    number: Plural]
                [Schema-spec t1665
                    slot: in*
                    filler:
                        [Schema-spec t1659
                            schema: FACE
                            number: Singular]]]]
```

Figure 4-25:   Case frame diagram for resolved ellipsis:
(Show me some flat bones) **In the face**

noun phrase added to the new noun phrase. This new noun phrase is then
acted on by the same rules as before, to produce the correct reference, and a
new resolved verb phrase that includes the new noun phrase.

The current handling of verb phrase ellipsis has two properties that allow
this treatment of constituent noun phrase ellipsis to work. The first is
simply that verb phrase ellipsis resolution must be based on sentence-local

case frames, and not their referents. The verb phrase must be resolved for the constituent noun phrase ellipsis to know which noun phrase to borrow its constituents from, but the referent of the noun phrase cannot be correctly determined until after the elided noun phrase constituents are resolved. The only way to do this if verb phrase ellipses were resolved based on their referents would be either to duplicate much of the ellipsis resolution effort or to create an incorrect reference and then later delete it. Both of these would be much more awkward.

The other necessary property is that once a noun phrase has been assigned to a verb phrase case, all of its descendant noun phrase states must be of that case, and any incorporation of a noun phrase into a verb phrase must respect the case of the noun phrase, if already assigned. This ensures that the noun phrase with the newly resolved constituents is incorporated into the same case that the constituents came from. In other words, without this restriction, a noun phrase could borrow a constituent from one antecedent noun phrase, and then replace a different antecedent noun phrase, which is clearly wrong. This restriction is enforced in two ways: the verb phrase ellipsis resolution rules cannot incorporate a noun phrase of different case from the case they produce; and there is yet another constraint propagation rule, which makes noun phrases inherit the case constraints of their ancestor verb phrases or noun phrases. Together these ensure the desired behavior.

The same rules can apply to noun phrase ellipses that occur in question-answer situations, in addition to the reformulation ellipsis shown here and the examples of correction and elaboration ellipsis given below, since these rules build up a normal noun phrase, which can then be handled by the usual verb phrase rules, the question context only affecting actions relating to verb phrase resolution.

4.4. Correction, elaboration, and dialogue charts

In this section, we present examples of correction and elaboration ellipsis resolution that are currently handled by the system. In addition to demonstrating the handling of these categories of ellipsis, these examples illustrate the ability of chart structures and actions to span sentence boundaries. We refer to the structure created in this way as a dialogue chart. If there are several competing interpretations for the individual sentences, and some are preferred due to their relationships with other sentences, the use of a chart can resolve sentential-level ambiguity just as it resolves ambiguity within a single sentence. This situation occurs in multiple "sentence" utterances, when a later utterance combines with an earlier one, as in a correction ellipsis.

4.4.1. Correction ellipsis

In the sequence

  Show Phil a rib for me
   RIB _ NUMBER _ 7
  Rich

the rules currently in the system will produce two ambiguous interpretations for the second utterance, one with *Rich* replacing *Phil*, and one with *Rich* replacing *me*. These two interpretations are shown in figures 4-26 and 4-27. However, if the sequence were

  Show Phil a rib for me
   RIB _ NUMBER _ 7
  Rich. For Rich

the system would interpret this as being an ambiguity correction, where the prepositional phrase is intended to replace the bare noun, disambiguating its case, and forcing the second interpretation. Although each elliptical utterance is individually ambiguous, the pair together is not, due to the relationship between them.

The chart for this correction ellipsis utterance is shown in figure 4-28. The only new system action shown here is the creation of state T0802 by a rule that says that if the antecedent of an ellipsis immediately precedes it in the same utterance, and the antecedent and the elliptical verb phrase are identical, then the verb phrase produced by the ellipsis resolution subsumes the antecedent. In this example, this causes the interpretation of *Rich* as the benefactor to be included with the interpretation of *For Rich* that has this as its antecedent as a request that spans the entire input utterance. This is significant because the rules that activate requests and questions, so that the system will respond to them, will only activate interpretations that span the full width of the utterance. Thus the spurious interpretation of *Rich*, and the spurious interpretation of *For Rich* as *To Rich for Rich*, are ignored, just as spurious constituents in a sentence are ignored when they are not included in the global sentence interpretation.

```
[Act-reference t0687
    action: Display
    mode: Imperative
    recip:
        [Reference t0765
            head: RHT
            deref: RHT]
    object: t0708
    bene: t0725
    deref: t0772]]

[Request t0778
    object:
        [Act t0772
            action: Display
            mode: Imperative
            recip: RHT
            object: t0717
            bene: BDF]]
```

Figure 4-26:   Case frame diagram for *(Show) Rich (a rib for me)*

```
[Act-reference t0687
    action: Display
    mode: Imperative
    recip: t0697
    object: t0708
    bene:
        [Reference t0765
            head: RHT
            deref: RHT]
    deref: t0769]]

[Request t0780
    object:
        [Act t0769
            action: Display
            mode: Imperative
            recip: PJH
            object: t0717
            bene: RHT]]
```

Figure 4-27:   Case frame diagram for *(Show Phil a rib for) Rich*

4.4.2. Elaboration ellipsis

Another type of multiple sentence utterance that is currently handled is an elaboration ellipsis, where an elliptical sentence adds additional information within the same utterance, as in

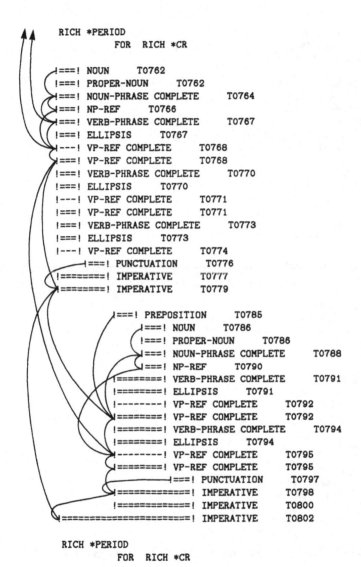

```
      RICH *PERIOD
              FOR   RICH *CR


   !===! NOUN      T0762
   !===! PROPER-NOUN        T0762
   !===! NOUN-PHRASE COMPLETE          T0764
   !===! NP-REF      T0766
   !===! VERB-PHRASE COMPLETE         T0767
   !===! ELLIPSIS      T0767
   !---! VP-REF  COMPLETE      T0768
   !===! VP-REF  COMPLETE      T0768
   !===! VERB-PHRASE COMPLETE         T0770
   !===! ELLIPSIS      T0770
   !---! VP-REF  COMPLETE      T0771
   !===! VP-REF  COMPLETE      T0771
   !===! VERB-PHRASE COMPLETE         T0773
   !===! ELLIPSIS      T0773
   !---! VP-REF  COMPLETE      T0774
        !===! PUNCTUATION      T0776
   !=======! IMPERATIVE        T0777
   !=======! IMPERATIVE        T0779


        !===! PREPOSITION       T0785
          !===! NOUN      T0786
          !===! PROPER-NOUN        T0786
          !===! NOUN-PHRASE COMPLETE        T0788
          !===! NP-REF       T0790
   !=========! VERB-PHRASE COMPLETE        T0791
   !=========! ELLIPSIS       T0791
   !---------! VP-REF COMPLETE       T0792
   !=========! VP-REF COMPLETE       T0792
   !=========! VERB-PHRASE COMPLETE        T0794
   !=========! ELLIPSIS       T0794
   !---------! VP-REF COMPLETE        T0795
   !=========! VP-REF COMPLETE        T0795
              !===! PUNCTUATION       T0797
   !=============! IMPERATIVE        T0798
   !=============! IMPERATIVE        T0800
   !=====================! IMPERATIVE        T0802


      RICH *PERIOD
              FOR   RICH *CR
```

Figure 4-28:   Chart built for a correction ellipsis

Display some long bones.   To Phil.

These are distinguished by the fact that there is no replacement of case
fillers, only extension or repetition. This allows both sentences to refer to the
same pending action, and so they are combined, as in the previous case.

There is an additional complication, because the lack of a replacement of a case cannot be checked in a single OPS5 rule. So the multiple sentence state is initially only proposed, and rules similar to the semantics checking rules check whether there are conflicting case role assignments, making the state posted and available to the other parsing rules only if no conflict is found.

A different situation holds where there is a case replacement, such as

Display some long bones. Some flat bones.

since here the two actions referred to cannot be the same. The second is either a replacement (correction) for the first action or a separate second action (reformulation). The safest course of action in a database retrieval situation is to assume that the second action is a separate action, and that the ellipsis is reformulation, unless there is a specific indication that the first action should be cancelled.

This presents a slight problem. Since the interpretation must be the width of the whole utterance in order to be activated, utterances that include several distinct sentences must somehow be linked together. This is done by a rule that builds a single state representing a multiple-sentence utterance, which has these sentences as its ancestors. The rules that activate utterances activate this full-width interpretation, and then, because it is not an actual sentence, activate its ancestors and then deactivate it again. If there are more than two sentences in an utterance, a tree of these states is built connecting them.

4.4.3. Dialogue charts

As shown in these examples, the semantic chart mechanism extends simply and naturally across sentence boundaries, when there is a clear, concrete relationship between sentences, such as coreference to a single action. It allows disambiguation of sentential-level ambiguity that would otherwise have to be done in a more *ad hoc* manner. This is a new use for the chart paradigm, made possible by the incorporation of semantics and reference relations into the chart. We believe it is a promising start towards utilizing levels of structure higher than sentences, as has been attempted with story-grammars [Rumelhart 75] and dialogue coherence [Hobbs 79].

The only occurrences of dialogue charts in this system are in multiple sentence utterances. Cross-sentence charts are probably more prevalent in monologues, since there one is building larger conceptual objects, such as paragraphs. In dialogues, it is our belief that the participants are not building a single conceptual object spanning both speakers' utterances, except for special situations where both parties already know how the other is likely to respond, as in theatrical performances, debates, or everyday word play and jokes.

4.5. The response phase

Once the goal of parsing is satisfied, a rule creates a goal of responding to the system's input. The first phase of the response is to mark all new user requests and questions as being active. This is described in detail in section 4.4 above, and is done in such a way that the oldest user input becomes the most recently touched, and therefore conflict resolution will make the system deal with multiple requests and questions in the order in which they occurred.

There can in general be a variety of actions in response to user commands. Given the database retrieval task, we have implemented two: displaying and halting. Halting is the simpler of the two, since it is an OPS5 primitive, so there is a single production that implements it[36]. This rule simply matches a request for a halt, creates a data structure indicating that the current action is the halt requested by the user in the last utterance and is a response to that utterance, marks the active request as being satisfied, prints *Good bye*, and then halts the system.

The display action is considerably more elaborate, requiring several dozen dedicated productions, summarized in table 4-3 and described below, and invoking a number of others previously described, such as semantic network searching rules. This complexity is caused by the variety of nominal descriptions that can occur within a display request: generics, singular, plural, universally quantified, etc.[37] In addition, wh-questions about sets are regarded as requests to display them.

---

[36]Implementing the response to a phrase like **stop** as a regular response action, rather than simply causing a halt within the parser, allows a very clean halt that can easily be restarted.

[37]In a system with a greater variety of actions, the productions for instantiating sets could be separated from those carrying out the specific action on a set element, thus preventing any combinatorial explosion in the number of productions.

display-recipient-checker—make sure recipient is known person
display-benefactor-checker—make sure benefactor is known person
display-object-checker—make sure object exists in database
display-generic-checker—make sure generic object is a class in database

display-generic-response—display a class
start-display-set-response—start display of set of objects
start-display-complex-set-response—start display of PP modified set
do-singular-display—display a singular set
do-singular-complex-display—display a singular, PP modified set
do-plural-display—start display of a plural set
do-complex-plural-display—start display of plural, PP modified set
finish-plural-display—stop plural display, enough facts displayed
finish-plural-display-1—stop plural display, out of candidates
finish-display-search—stop search if display is done
do-universal-display—display elements of a universal set
do-complex-universal-display—display elements of PP modified universal set
finish-universal-display—stop universal display, out of elements

bad-display-set-response—there is no "other" set
empty-display-set-response—nothing to display

be-actor-checker—make sure "actor" is a wh-phrase
be-object-checker—make sure "object" is in database

start-wh-q-be-response—start response to a wh-question
intersect-set—create a set that is an intersection of other sets
end-intersect-set—done elaborating intersection set
bad-wh-q-response—question is improperly phrased

end-full-search—turn off search when nothing more available
make-set-yes—mark fact's set membership, if not redundant
make-set-no—do not mark redundant set membership
give-fact-nil-superset—every fact needs at least a nil superset
remove-redundant-nil-superset—remove nil superset if not needed
reset-facts—make displayed facts displayable again
display-set-response—record that we displayed an object
request-response-actor—records the system as the actor in requests

Table 4-3:   Rules written for display action

The display of a generic, as in

Show me the rib
RIB
(INSTANCES (VALUE FALSE_RIB TRUE_RIB))
(IS-A (VALUE LONG_BONE))
(LOCATED-IN (VALUE TRUNK))

is relatively simple, since no searching is necessary. A single rule simply displays the frame called for, using a Common Lisp function, and then records the same sort of information that the halt response does. This rule is shown in figure 4-29, with an English translation in figure 4-30.

For displays of sets of frames, the response starts with a production that recognizes that a display of a set is called for. There are currently two of these productions, one for a set without a prepositional phrase, and one for a set with a locative prepositional phrase. Each of these creates a pair of goals, one to carry out a semantic network search and one to display the set. The network search locates and loads the frames satisfying the description, using the same productions that carry out network searches elsewhere. The action of the two goals is interleaved, in that the actual display productions can fire during the search, and the search is terminated as soon as the display goal is satisfied.

For example, if the system is carrying out the response

Display an irregular bone
THORACIC_VERTEBRA
(IS-A (VALUE VERTEBRA))

the production "do-singular-display" would fire as soon as the first leaf[38] frame matching this description was loaded into working memory. This rule displays the frame it matches, and then marks the display goal as satisfied and the fact representing the *is-a** of the frame as having been displayed as the concrete instantiation of this set. This marking of facts as members of sets is crucial, so that later references can know exactly which frames were chosen in response to earlier indefinite requests. The marking of the goal as

---

[38]The semantic database being used in this application makes no distinction between instances and classes, so the display productions were constructed using the assumption that leaf nodes correspond to instances.

```
(p display-generic-response
    { (goal ^status active ^name respond)        <grespond> }
    { (request ^token <ctok> ^object <dtok> ^utt <u>
                ^status active)                  <concept> }
    (act ^action display ^token <dtok> ^recip <rec> ^bene <ben>
        ^object <obj>)
    (schema-spec ^set <obj> ^schema { <schema> <> nil } )

;;; Find action we're responding to
    (act ^action speak ^object <u> ^token <a>)
    { (action ^token <olda> ^action <a> ^state <oldstate>)
                                                 <action> }
    (word-seq ^first <oldp> ^state <oldstate>)

    { (word-cnt ^word <w>)                       <wordcnt> }
    { (utt-cnt ^utt <n>)                         <uttcnt> }
    -->
;;; Record the fact that we responded
    (bind <act> (gint)) (bind <new-state> (gint))
    (bind <new-state-2> (gint))
    (bind <w1> (compute <w> + 1))
    (bind <n1> (compute <n> + 1))

    (make dialogue-relation ^relation response ^relator <act>
        ^relatee <olda> ^state <new-state-2> ^utt <n1>)
    (make word-seq ^first <oldp> ^last <w1> ^state <new-state-2>
                ^utt <n1>)

    (make word-seq ^first <w1> ^state <new-state> ^utt <n1>)
    (modify <wordcnt> ^word <w1>)
    (modify <uttcnt> ^utt <n1>)
    (modify <action> ^next <act>)
    (make action ^token <act> ^action <dtok> ^prev <olda>
                ^state <new-state> ^utt <n1>)

    (modify <concept> ^status satisfied)
    (write (crlf))
    (call ps-ppf <schema>)
    (write (crlf)))
```

Figure 4-29:   Production rule for displaying generics

satisfied terminates this display action. A similar rule works for displays of
singular sets with locative descriptions attached to them, as in

> *Display an irregular bone in the face*
> **PALATE**
> **(IS-A (VALUE IRREGULAR_BONE))**
> **(PART-OF (VALUE FACE))**
> **(BILATERAL (VALUE T))**

RULE display-generic-response:
IF   there is an active goal to respond
        and there is an active request from utterance <u>
              and action <dtok>
        and action <dtok> is a display action of <obj>
        and object <obj> is simply the frame <schema>
        and action <a> produced this utterance
        and action <a> was described by <olda> in state <oldstate>
        and the first word of this action was <oldp>
        and we are currently at word <w>
        and we are currently at utterance <n>
THEN   obtain unique names for a new act and two new states
        compute the new current word and current utterance
        build an indication that the new act is a response to <olda>
        give this description a location (for display purposes)
        produce a location for the new (display) action
        update the current word count
        update the current utterance count
        link the new action into the list of actions
        build a description of the new action
        indicate that this request is now satisfied
        output a display of the frame <schema>

Figure 4-30:   English version of rule for displaying generics

Both of these rules, and all other display rules, check to make sure there is
no "other-than" set descriptor matching any set the fact belongs to. This
prevents a phrase such as *another irregular bone* from being acted upon
until a new irregular bone not already displayed is loaded. After the display
goal is satisfied, a rule marks each of the facts as available for display again,
leaving their set affiliation alone.

If an unquantified, plural display were called for, as in

Display irregular bones
    THORACIC_VERTEBRA
    (IS-A (VALUE VERTEBRA))

    SACRAL_VERTEBRA
    (IS-A (VALUE VERTEBRA))
    (PART-OF (VALUE SACRUM))

    LUMBAR_VERTEBRA
    (IS-A (VALUE VERTEBRA))

a similar rule fires, which displays the frame it matches, and then decrements a count[39] of frames displayed, rather than marking the goal as satisfied. When this count reaches zero, or the network search cannot find any more frames matching the set descriptor, the display goal is marked as satisfied by another rule, again terminating the display action. As in all other cases, there is a second rule that handles the situation if a locative description is attached to the set descriptor.

In the case of a universally quantified object, such as

Display all the true ribs
     RIB_NUMBER_7
     RIB_NUMBER_6
     RIB_NUMBER_5
     RIB_NUMBER_4
     RIB_NUMBER_3
     RIB_NUMBER_2
     RIB_NUMBER_1

the display rule simply displays the name of each matching frame as it appears, and marks it as displayed. When there are no more frames to display, a different rule marks the display goal as satisfied.

In contrast to successful set displays, a request for an obviously ill-formed set of objects can be almost as simple to handle as a generic display, since once again no search is required. In situations where the user asks, e.g.,

Display another irregular bone

and no irregular bones have been displayed yet, a set description is created during the parse that indicates that there is no "other-than" set. This causes a response rule to fire that prints out the error message

Sorry but there is no previous IRREGULAR_BONE

and then marks the goal of displaying the set as satisfied. There are two such rules, one for requests and one for wh-questions.

The final rule to fire in a set display is one of a pair, depending on whether the display response succeeded in finding any frames to display. Both rules record all the information that the generic display rule in figure 4-29 does, but one rule also prints out an error message, for example

---

[39]This count is currently arbitrarily initialized to three objects.

Sorry but there is no such TRUE_RIB

This "empty-display-set-response" rule fires in the case where there is no fact marked as having been displayed as part of the current set. Both rules mark the request as having been answered, and delete the goal of displaying the set.

The response to wh-questions starts with a rule similar to the ones that start displays of sets. It recognizes wh-questions involving the verb *be*[40], as in

> *Which ribs are true ribs?*
> RIB_NUMBER_1
> RIB_NUMBER_2
> RIB_NUMBER_3
> RIB_NUMBER_4
> RIB_NUMBER_5
> RIB_NUMBER_6
> RIB_NUMBER_7

and creates four goals: two to find all members of the source sets, one to create a new set consisting of the intersection of the two source sets, and another to display the resulting set. The first two goals are handled by network searching rules; the display goal is handled by the previously discussed display rules. The set intersection goal, however, requires two new productions. The main one looks for a single schema with fact elements indicating that it is in both source sets. If this schema is not in a set that should be "other-than" the new one, a new fact is created indicating that this schema is in the intersection set. The other rule simply deletes the set intersection goal when no other set rules can act.

---

[40]Responses to other forms of wh-questions could be added simply by adding rules that understood the semantics of other verbs, or other uses of **be**.

4.6. Future chart developments

One change that clearly should be made is to re-write the system to separate the mechanics of case frame manipulation from the syntactic rules about how surface cases work in English. This would permit easier extension and modification of the system, and allow greater clarity in the phrasing of the rules. It would be similar to the current separation between the rules that manipulate semantic network frames and sets, the rules that carry out domain-dependent semantic checking and actions, and the rest of the rules. This type of separation allows modular specification of different kinds of rules without sacrificing integrated functioning of different types of rules during actual processing.

Other future developments include the handling of deep case frames that extend across more than one sentence and meta-language utterances. Some of the ground work for these has already been laid; they are discussed in detail in chapter 6.

The next chapter consists of a long, detailed trace of an example dialogue, with copious additional annotations. Several inputs and outputs will be covered, in an attempt to make the fine-grain behavior of the system clear.

Chapter 5
The Program in Action

5.1. Introduction

This chapter presents a detailed trace of an interaction between the Psli3 system and a user. The domain of the system is a medical database. A synopsis of the interaction is shown in figure 5-1. The chart diagram for the parse of each utterance is given at the beginning of the section presenting its trace.

The first utterance is a normal sentence, setting the context for the rest of the dialogue. The system responds with the requested action, and then the user uses an elliptical sentence to request another display. The new rib is displayed. The user then asks for the same bone to be displayed to someone else, using a form of constituent ellipsis. Notice that this fragment is actually syntactically ambiguous, since it could be a request to show Mark to someone. Both interpretations are proposed by the syntactic rules, and then the incorrect one is rejected by the semantics checking rules. This prevents it from being acted on further. The correct interpretation succeeds, and the appropriate display action is done. The final request is a bit more complicated, due to the use of an "other" reference, and the presence of two cases of an elided verb phrase.

Display a sternal rib to Phil
    RIB_NUMBER_7
    (IS-A (VALUE TRUE_RIB))
A floating rib
    RIB_NUMBER_12
    (IS-A (VALUE FLOATING_RIB))
Show Mark.
    RIB_NUMBER_12
    (IS-A (VALUE FLOATING_RIB))
Another sternal rib to me.
    RIB_NUMBER_1
    (IS-A (VALUE TRUE_RIB))

Figure 5-1: Interaction between Psli3 and user

A detailed trace showing virtually all the rule firings[41] and the most interesting working memory elements follows below. The numbering of the rule firings indicates the order that the firings happened to occur in, as the rules in OPS5 have no inherent static ordering. In the current system, implemented in OPS5 under Common Lisp on a Symbolics 3600 Lisp Machine, there are about 225 production rules statically defined, plus 30 lexicon frames in the semantic network, each of which generates from two to nine lexicon rules at system load time. There are also 9 frames defining people the system knows, all of which are handled by one general name rule. The total number of rules at run time at the moment is 361. A typical sentence is interpreted in about one minute, when tracing is off. This is too slow for actual use as an interface, by a factor of about ten. Note that this time includes all parses generated, disambiguation, and semantic interpretation, and so cannot be compared to the time a purely syntactic parser takes to produce a single parse tree.

---

[41]In a few cases where the firings are extremely repetitive, only the first and last are shown. These are clearly marked.

5.2. The initial full sentence

The chart diagram for the first sentence is presented in figure 5-2. This is an ordinary imperative sentence, used to set the context for the remaining dialogue.

```
DISPLAY
        A       STERNAL
                        RIB   TO     PHIL *CR

!===! VERB-PHRASE 2        T0042
!===! VERB       T0042
!===! VERB-PHRASE 1        T0049
!===! VERB       T0049
!===! VP-REF 1        T0053
        !===! DETERMINER        T0055
        !===! NOUN-PHRASE        T0057
             !===! NP-NULL        T0059
                  !===! NOUN        T0060
             !========! NOUN        T0066
        !=============! NOUN-PHRASE COMPLETE        T0076
        !=============! NP-REF        T0077
!=================! VERB-PHRASE COMPLETE        T0079
!------------------! VP-REF COMPLETE        T0080
!=================! VP-REF COMPLETE        T0080
                        !===! PREPOSITION        T0082
                             !===! NOUN        T0083
                             !===! PROPER-NOUN        T0083
                             !===! NOUN-PHRASE COMPLETE        T0085
                             !===! NP-REF        T0087
!============================! VERB-PHRASE COMPLETE        T0088
!---------------------------! VP-REF COMPLETE        T0089
!============================! VP-REF COMPLETE        T0089
                             !===! PUNCTUATION        T0091
!==================================! IMPERATIVE        T0092

Ready to assemble a meaning for state T0092

    RIB_NUMBER_7
        (IS-A (VALUE TRUE_RIB))

                                !===! DISPLAY        T0097
!======================================! RESPONSE        T0098
!======================================! DIALOGUE-SEG        T0099
```

Figure 5-2:   Chart of first sentence in dialogue

Rule firings:

(run)
1. START-UP
2. START-GOALS
3. GORO-PUSH-POSTED-GOAL-FIRST-
                              SUBGOAL
4. GORO-ACTIVATE-POSTED-TERMINAL-
                              GOAL
5. MESS-CLEANED-UP
6. GORO-POP-AND-OR-AND*-SUCCESS
7. GORO-PUSH-SUBGOALED-GOAL-NEXT-
                              SUBGOAL
8. GORO-ACTIVATE-POSTED-TERMINAL-
                              GOAL
9. GET-INPUT

+ display a sternal rib to phil

The first two rules load initial information and initial goals into working memory. The goals are arranged in a hierarchy that indicates what sequence they should be applied in. The next two rules then select and activate the goal of deleting obsolete working memory elements. Since there are no old elements yet, the rule terminating clean-up fires. The next three rules select and activate the goal for getting user input. This causes the rule that actual gets the input to fire.

Input states:

71: (INPUT ^WORD DISPLAY ^POSITION
     1 ^NEXT 2 ^UTT T ^PREV 0 ^END
     LEFT ^UTT-END LEFT ^STATE
     I0039)
72: (STATE ^STATUS POSTED ^UTT 1
     ^STATE I0039)
69: (INPUT ^WORD A ^POSITION 2
     ^NEXT 3 ^UTT T ^PREV 1 ^STATE
     I0038)
70: (STATE ^STATUS POSTED ^UTT 1
     ^STATE I0038)
67: (INPUT ^WORD STERNAL ^POSITION
     3 ^NEXT 4 ^UTT T ^PREV 2
     ^STATE I0037)
68: (STATE ^STATUS POSTED ^UTT 1
     ^STATE I0037)

The input reading rule uses a Common Lisp function to input the user's utterance and place the individual words into states in working memory. These states are shown here, along with the utterance and word counters used to keep track of the current position in the dialogue.

The numbers on the left are the time-stamp numbers that OPS5 assigns to every working memory element created, in order of creation. The numbers run backwards here because the input states are placed in working memory from right to

65: (INPUT ^WORD RIB ^POSITION 4
     ^NEXT 5 ^UTT T ^PREV 3 ^STATE
     I0036)

66: (STATE ^STATUS POSTED ^UTT 1
     ^STATE I0036)

63: (INPUT ^WORD TO ^POSITION 5
     ^NEXT 6 ^UTT T ^PREV 4 ^STATE
     I0035)

64: (STATE ^STATUS POSTED ^UTT 1
     ^STATE I0035)

61: (INPUT ^WORD PHIL ^POSITION 6
     ^NEXT 7 ^UTT T ^PREV 5 ^STATE
     I0034)

62: (STATE ^STATUS POSTED ^UTT 1
     ^STATE I0034)

59: (INPUT ^WORD *CR ^POSITION 7
     ^NEXT 8 ^UTT T ^PREV 6 ^END
     RIGHT ^UTT-END RIGHT ^STATE
     I0033)

60: (STATE ^STATUS POSTED ^UTT 1
     ^STATE I0033)

56: (UTT-CNT ^UTT 1)
58: (WORD-CNT ^WORD 7)

left. This was originally done to cause left-to-right parsing based on recency, although now an explicit mechanism ensures left-to-right parsing without depending on recency, using the ^UTT attribute of INPUT elements, which is later used for the utterance number.

The attributes ^END and ^UTT-END mark the ends of the sentence and the whole utterance, respectively, since an utterance may consist of more than one sentence.

The input reading rule also creates some working memory elements, not shown here, indicating that this is an action by the speaker, and marks the goal of getting input as satisfied.

Rule firings:

10. GORO-POP-AND-OR-AND*-SUCCESS
11. GORO-PUSH-SUBGOALED-GOAL-NEXT-
                              SUBGOAL
12. GORO-ACTIVATE-POSTED-TERMINAL-
                                GOAL
13. START-UNDERSTAND
14. GET-FIRST-WORD
15. DICT-DISPLAY
16. DICT-DISPLAY-IMP

The next four rules select and activate the goal for parsing the input. Then GET-FIRST-WORD fires, which changes the ^UTT attribute of the first INPUT element from T to NIL. This activates the first word, starting the left-to-right input activation mentioned above.

Two lexicon rules fire, placing two definitions for DISPLAY into working memory, in two different states. The first defines the declarative form, the second the imperative form

17. IMPERATIVE-VERB-REF

Verb phrase reference state:

```
111: (STATE ^STATUS POSTED ^UTT 1
     ^STATE T0053)
112: (POS ^CON T0049 ^STATUS 1
     ^TYPE VP-REF ^STATE T0053)
113: (ANCESTOR ^ANCESTOR T0048
     ^STATE T0053)
114: (ACT ^TOKEN T0054 ^ACTION
     DISPLAY ^MODE IMP ^STATE
     T0053 ^E-SUBJ T)
115: (ACT-REFERENCE ^TOKEN T0049
     ^ACTION DISPLAY ^MODE IMP
     ^STATE T0053 ^DEREF T0054
     ^E-SUBJ T)
116: (WORD-SEQ ^FIRST 1 ^LAST 1
     ^NEXT 2 ^PREV 0 ^STATE T0053)
```

of the verb. The state created by the second lexicon rule during a different run was shown in figure 4-4 on page 53. These coexist without interfering with each other, as do all local ambiguities.

Because imperative verbs' referents can simply be created without search, the existence of the syntactic verb phrase causes the rule that creates the initial referent for imperative verbs to fire, creating the state shown here.

The ACT element is the beginning of the case frame representing the action referred to by the imperative verb.

The ACT-REFERENCE element is a copy of the ACT-REFERENCE in the verb phrase created by the lexicon rule, T0049, with the ^DEREF attribute set to T0054, the referent of the verb phrase, which is this state's ACT. The attribute E-SUBJ is T to indicate that the subject case of this verb phrase is not available.

The STATE element carries information about which utterance this is part of, and whether the state as a whole is available for parsing (POSTED) or only PROPOSED.

The ANCESTOR element indicates the states that this state is based on, and is used primarily at the end of the parse, to locate all states that contributed to the correct interpretation.

The POS elements indicate the syntactic categories this state is a member of. The ^STATUS attribute indicates, for verb phrases, the number of required cases not yet filled.

Finally, the WORD-SEQ element indicates the location of this state in the chart. This is the information used by rules that combine states to determine whether two states are contiguous.

```
Rule firings and wm changes:

18. AFTERMATH 89 91
=>wm:
117: (GOAL ^NAME
     CP-NOTICE-SITUATION ^STATUS
     ACTIVE ^SPEC 1)


19. NEXT-WORD 117 91 69
<=wm:
69: (INPUT ^WORD A ^POSITION 2
     ^NEXT 3 ^UTT T ^PREV 1 ^STATE
     I0038)
=>wm:
119: (INPUT ^WORD A ^POSITION 2
     ^NEXT 3 ^PREV 1 ^STATE I0038)
<=wm:
117: (GOAL ^NAME
     CP-NOTICE-SITUATION ^STATUS
     ACTIVE ^SPEC 1)
```

AFTERMATH fires when no other parsing rule can fire, creating a goal called CP-NOTICE-SITUATION that indicates that fact. This allows rules such as error detection to fire after all the regular parsing rules are finished. (In this more detailed type of trace, the time-stamps of the elements matched by a rule are shown to the right of its name; its additions to working memory are marked by =>wm: and its deletions from working memory are marked by <=wm:)

Since no such rules match here, NEXT-WORD fires immediately. This rule activates the word following the current word and removes the CP-NOTICE-SITUATION goal.

Rule firings:

20. DICT-A
21. DET-NEW-NP

New noun phrase state:

125: (STATE ^STATUS POSTED ^UTT 1
       ^STATE T0057)
126: (ANCESTOR ^ANCESTOR T0055
       ^STATE T0057)
127: (POS ^CON T0058 ^TYPE
       NOUN-PHRASE ^STATE T0057)
128: (REFERENCE ^TOKEN T0058 ^DET
       INDEF ^STATE T0057 ^QUANT T)
130: (WORD-SEQ ^FIRST 2 ^LAST 2
       ^NEXT 3 ^PREV 1 ^STATE T0057)

Now that the word *a* is available, its lexicon rule fires, loading its definition into working memory. This is simply a state at position 2 in the input with a POS element indicating an indefinite determiner.

The presence of this state allows the rule to fire that creates new noun phrases when determiners not preceded by quantifiers are seen. It creates a REFERENCE case frame for a new noun phrase, with an indefinite determiner (^DET) attribute. The ^QUANT attribute is set to T to indicate that the quantifier case should not be filled, since quantifiers should not appear to the right of the determiner.

Rule firings:

22. AFTERMATH
23. NEXT-WORD
24. DICT-TRUE_RIB-2-FLUSH1

The word *sternal* is the first word of the idiomatic phrase *sternal rib*, so a lexicon rule fires to indicate that this is a known word with no associated semantics. This lexicon rule is named DICT-TRUE_RIB-2-FLUSH1 because sternal ribs can also be called *true ribs*.

25. AFTERMATH
26. NEXT-WORD
27. DICT-RIB-S

The system moves on to the next word, *rib*, so the lexicon rule fires that loads the definition of this word into working memory.

28. PCONCEPTG-YES

Lexicon rules for nouns also create DO-PCONCEPTG goals, requesting that their frames be loaded into working memory. This goal mechanism ensures that the frame will only get loaded if it is not already present in working memory. Since the RIB frame is not, PCONCEPTG-YES loads the frame and deletes the goal.

29. DICT-TRUE_RIB-2-S

"Sternal rib" state:

153: (STATE ^STATUS POSTED ^UTT 1
      ^STATE T0066)
154: (ANCESTOR ^ANCESTOR I0037
      ^STATE T0066)
155: (ANCESTOR ^ANCESTOR I0036
      ^STATE T0066)
157: (POS ^CON T0067 ^TYPE NOUN
      ^STATE T0066 ^NUMBER SINGULAR
      ^OBJECT TRUE_RIB)
158: (WORD-SEQ ^FIRST 3 ^LAST 4
      ^NEXT 5 ^PREV 2 ^STATE T0066)

Since both its words have been activated, the lexicon rule for *sternal rib* fires, placing a definition of that phrase in working memory, and requesting the corresponding frame to be loaded. This state has two ancestor states, since it was created due to the presence of two words. The ^OBJECT attribute indicates the internal name of the semantic network frame that this noun refers to.

Rule firings:

30. PCONCEPTG-YES

Since this frame is not present yet either, PCONCEPTG-YES loads it too.

True_rib frame in wm:

159: (FACT ^ID T0068 ^SCHEMA
      TRUE_RIB ^SLOT INSTANCES
      ^FILLER RIB_NUMBER_1)

```
160: (FACT ^ID T0069 ^SCHEMA
      TRUE_RIB ^SLOT INSTANCES
      ^FILLER RIB_NUMBER_2)
161: (FACT ^ID T0070 ^SCHEMA
      TRUE_RIB ^SLOT INSTANCES
      ^FILLER RIB_NUMBER_3)
162: (FACT ^ID T0071 ^SCHEMA
      TRUE_RIB ^SLOT INSTANCES
      ^FILLER RIB_NUMBER_4)
163: (FACT ^ID T0072 ^SCHEMA
      TRUE_RIB ^SLOT INSTANCES
      ^FILLER RIB_NUMBER_5)
164: (FACT ^ID T0073 ^SCHEMA
      TRUE_RIB ^SLOT INSTANCES
      ^FILLER RIB_NUMBER_6)
165: (FACT ^ID T0074 ^SCHEMA
      TRUE_RIB ^SLOT INSTANCES
      ^FILLER RIB_NUMBER_7)
166: (FACT ^ID T0075 ^SCHEMA
      TRUE_RIB ^SLOT IS-A ^FILLER
      RIB)
```

Rule firings:

31. NOUN-OLD-NP

This rule takes a noun and adds it to a noun phrase that has already been started by another word. It makes a copy of the REFERENCE working memory element representing the noun phrase, and adds a ^HEAD attribute to it, indicating the frame that the head noun of the noun phrase refers to.

32. INDEFINITE-NP-REF-1

Referent state:

174: (STATE ^STATUS POSTED ^UTT 1
      ^STATE T0077)
175: (POS ^CON T0058 ^TYPE NP-REF
      ^STATE T0077)
176: (ANCESTOR ^ANCESTOR T0076
      ^STATE T0077)
177: (REFERENCE ^TOKEN T0058 ^DET
      INDEF ^HEAD TRUE_RIB ^STATE
      T0077 ^NUMBER SINGULAR ^QUANT
      T ^DEREF T0078)
178: (SCHEMA-SPEC ^SET T0078 ^SLOT
      IS-A* ^FILLER TRUE_RIB ^STATE
      T0077 ^NUMBER SINGULAR)
179: (WORD-SEQ ^FIRST 2 ^LAST 4
      ^NEXT 5 ^PREV 1 ^STATE T0077)

Now that there is an indefinite noun phrase with a head, a referent-building rule fires, creating the set descriptor SCHEMA-SPEC for a set of ribs with one element. If this were a definite reference, the system would have had to find an old set matching the noun phrase's description. The reference relationship between the noun phrase and this new set is indicated by the ^DEREF attribute of the modified REFERENCE element copied from the syntactic noun phrase state.

Rule firings:

33. E-UNMARKED-2ND

Verb phrase state:

180: (STATE ^STATUS POSTED ^UTT 1
      ^STATE T0079)
181: (POS ^CON T0049 ^TYPE
      VERB-PHRASE ^STATE T0079)
182: (ANCESTOR ^ANCESTOR T0048
      ^STATE T0079)
183: (ANCESTOR ^ANCESTOR T0076
      ^STATE T0079)
184: (ACT-REFERENCE ^TOKEN T0049
      ^ACTION DISPLAY ^MODE IMP
      ^STATE T0079 ^OBJECT T0058
      ^E-SUBJ T ^E-2ND T)

The existence of the noun phrase (state T0076) immediately following the initial verb phrase (state T0048) allows a rule to fire that adds a direct object, or second object, to a verb phrase that can accept a second object but does not have one yet. This is placed in the ^OBJECT slot of the ACT-REFERENCE, and ^E-2ND is set to T to indicate that the second object surface case is filled. Both the surface and deep cases were indicated by an EXPECT element in the original verb frame, shown on a different run in figure 4-4 on page 53.

185: (CONSTRAINT ^ELEMENT T0049
      ^TYPE CASE ^SLOT OBJECT
      ^FILLER T0058 ^STATE T0079)
186: (WORD-SEQ ^FIRST 1 ^LAST 4
      ^NEXT 5 ^PREV 0 ^STATE T0079)

Rule firings:

34. REDUCED-VP
35. DONE-VP

The CONSTRAINT element redundantly indicates that this noun phrase fills this case, in order to work around restrictions in the way OPS5 rules match working memory. This CONSTRAINT element will be propagated to all verb phrases descended from this state, indicating that this case is not allowed to be refilled. This does not prevent a parallel verb phrase with a different filler of this case from being created, when appropriate.

REDUCED-VP subtracts one from the number of required cases unfilled in the parent verb phrase state to get the number still unfilled in the new verb phrase state. In this case, the number is zero, which causes DONE-VP to fire, marking the POS element's ^STATUS as COMPLETE.

---

36. CONTINUE-VP-REF

Verb phrase state:

195: (STATE ^STATUS PROPOSED ^UTT 1
      ^SPEC OBJECT ^STATE T0080)
196: (POS ^CON T0049 ^STATUS
      COMPLETE ^TYPE VP-REF ^STATE
      T0080)
197: (ANCESTOR ^ANCESTOR T0079
      ^STATE T0080)
198: (ANCESTOR ^ANCESTOR T0053
      ^STATE T0080)
199: (ANCESTOR ^ANCESTOR T0077
      ^STATE T0080)

Since we have a verb phrase with a new syntactic case filler that has a referent, and the ancestor of that verb phrase has a verb phrase referent, the rule that builds a larger verb phrase referent from a smaller one now fires. It proposes that the deep case corresponding to the newly filled surface case be filled with the referent of the noun phrase. Since this requires possibly complex semantic checking, the STATE is indicated as being PROPOSED, with the case in question indicated by the ^SPEC attribute.

```
200:  (ACT ^TOKEN T0081 ^ACTION
       DISPLAY ^MODE IMP ^STATE
       T0080 ^OBJECT T0078
       ^E-SUBJ T)
201:  (ACT-REFERENCE ^TOKEN T0049
       ^ACTION DISPLAY ^MODE IMP
       ^STATE T0080 ^OBJECT T0058
       ^DEREF T0081 ^E-SUBJ T
       ^E-2ND T)
202:  (WORD-SEQ ^FIRST 1 ^LAST 4
       ^NEXT 5 ^PREV 0 ^STATE T0080)
```

Rule firings:

37. CONSTRAINT-PROPAGATION
38. DISPLAY-OBJECT-CHECKER

---

39. AFTERMATH
40. NEXT-WORD
41. DICT-PREP
42. AFTERMATH
43. NEXT-WORD
44. DICT-NAME
45. NOUN-NEW-NP
46. DEREF-NAME

Referent noun phrase state:

```
229:  (STATE ^STATUS POSTED ^UTT 1
       ^STATE T0087)
230:  (POS ^CON T0086 ^TYPE NP-REF
       ^STATE T0087)
231:  (ANCESTOR ^ANCESTOR T0085
       ^STATE T0087)
```

CONSTRAINT-PROPAGATION fires, creating a copy of the earlier CONSTRAINT element in the new state, so that the case filled previously cannot be refilled.

The existence of a proposed display of an object causes the semantics checking rule associated with objects of display actions to fire, indicating that this action is acceptable by modifying the STATE element to POSTED. This is how semantic acceptability influences the parsing process. This particular check simply involves making sure that there are database objects of the type referred to by the noun phrase.

The system moves on to the next word, which is *to*. This is recognized by a lexical rule that handles all prepositions known to the system, which creates a state representing it.

The system moves on again, to create a state for *Phil* using a rule that recognizes all names known to the system.

This state allows a rule to fire (rule firing 45) that creates a new noun phrase for a noun not preceded by a determiner or quantifier.

232: (REFERENCE ^TOKEN T0086 ^DET T
     ^HEAD PJH ^STATE T0087 ^QUANT
     T ^DEREF PJH)
233: (WORD-SEQ ^FIRST 6 ^LAST 6
     ^NEXT 7 ^PREV 5 ^STATE T0087)

The referent for the noun phase is then determined (firing 46), by a rule that creates referent descriptions for names.

Rule firings:

47. E-MARKED
48. PROPAGATE-UNREDUCED-VP
49. CONTINUE-VP-REF

Verb phrase referent state:

246: (STATE ^STATUS PROPOSED ^UTT 1
     ^SPEC RECIP ^STATE T0089)
247: (POS ^CON T0049 ^STATUS
     COMPLETE ^TYPE VP-REF ^STATE
     T0089)
248: (ANCESTOR ^ANCESTOR T0088
     ^STATE T0089)
249: (ANCESTOR ^ANCESTOR T0080
     ^STATE T0089)
250: (ANCESTOR ^ANCESTOR T0087
     ^STATE T0089)
251: (ACT ^TOKEN T0090 ^ACTION
     DISPLAY ^MODE IMP ^STATE
     T0089 ^RECIP PJH ^OBJECT
     T0078 ^E-SUBJ T)
252: (ACT-REFERENCE ^TOKEN T0049
     ^ACTION DISPLAY ^MODE IMP
     ^STATE T0089 ^RECIP T0086
     ^OBJECT T0058 ^DEREF T0090
     ^E-SUBJ T ^E-2ND T)
253: (WORD-SEQ ^FIRST 1 ^LAST 6
     ^NEXT 7 ^PREV 0 ^STATE T0089)

The presence of the preposition and the noun phrase states after the verb phrase state allows a rule to fire that adds marked cases onto verb phrases, in a fashion very similar to E-UNMARKED-2ND, in rule firing number 33.

This new verb phrase then is marked as syntactically COMPLETE, since its ancestor already had all its required cases.

The rule for continuing verb phrase referents fires again, creating another proposed referent verb phrase, this time filling the recipient case with the internal name for Phil.

CONSTRAINT-PROPAGATION fires twice (next page), propagating constraints for both the object case and the recipient case.

The semantics checking rule for the recipient of a display requires the recipient to be a person known to the system. Since this is satisfied, the rule fires, marking the state as posted, thus allowing the other parsing rules to act on it.

Rule firings:

50. CONSTRAINT-PROPAGATION
51. CONSTRAINT-PROPAGATION
52. DISPLAY-RECIPIENT-CHECKER
53. CONSTRAINT-PROPAGATION

A somewhat delayed propagation of a constraint then occurs, propagating the constraint on the object case into the verb phrase created by E-MARKED.

54. AFTERMATH
55. NEXT-WORD
56. DICT-PUNCT
57. REQUEST-SENTENCE

Request state:

267: (STATE ^STATUS POSTED ^UTT 1
     ^STATE T0092)
268: (POS ^CON T0093 ^TYPE
     IMPERATIVE ^STATE T0092)
269: (ANCESTOR ^ANCESTOR T0089
     ^STATE T0092)
270: (ANCESTOR ^ANCESTOR T0091
     ^STATE T0092)
271: (REQUEST ^TOKEN T0093 ^STATE
     T0092 ^OBJECT T0090)
272: (WORD-SEQ ^FIRST 1 ^LAST 7
     ^NEXT 8 ^PREV 0 ^STATE T0092)

The system moves on to the next word, which is actually a carriage return, represented internally as *CR. The presence of an end-of-sentence punctuation at the end of an imperative verb phrase that has a referent and no missing required cases allows the rule that builds request full sentences to fire.

Rule firings:

58. AFTERMATH
59. LAST-WORD
60. PARSING-FINISHED
61. GORO-POP-AND-OR-AND*-SUCCESS
62. GORO-PUSH-SUBGOALED-GOAL-NEXT-
                          SUBGOAL

The system prepares to move on to another word, but there are no more. LAST-WORD reacts to the situation by creating the goal CP-FINAL-SITUATION. Since we are at the end of the input and there is a single state that describes the whole input, we have succeeded in parsing the input, so

```
63. GORO-ACTIVATE-POSTED-TERMINAL-
                               GOAL
64. FIND-FINAL-STATE-1
65. INSTALL-TOP-OBJECTS

    <A large number of firings
    of Install-Other-Objects
    and Install-Top-Objects>

159. INSTALL-TOP-OBJECTS
160. ASSEMBLY-DONE
161. GORO-POP-LAST-AND-OR-AND*-
                            SUCCESS
162. GORO-STOP-CLEANING-SUCCEEDED-
                               GOAL
163. PARSE-SUCCESS
164. ACTIVATE-REQUESTS
165. START-RESPOND
```

PARSING-FINISHED fires, which marks the parsing goals as SUCCEEDED and deletes CP-FINAL-SITUATION.

The goal rules then select and activate the goal CP-ASSEMBLE, which causes the system to back-trace from the final state and mark all states that are part of the correct parse. FIND-FINAL-STATE-1 starts this process, by marking the STATE of the final state as ^STATUS PERMANENT.

The two rules INSTALL-TOP-OBJECTS and INSTALL-OTHER-OBJECTS do the actual back-tracing. The former marks all elements of the top state; the latter marks all elements in states that are ancestors of a marked state. The marking consists of setting the ^UTT attribute of non-STATE elements to the current utterance number.

Once this is done, ASSEMBLY-DONE marks the goal as SUCCEEDED, and the goal rules and PARSE-SUCCESS select and activate the goal START-RESPOND, starting the response phase. This allows ACTIVATE-REQUESTS to mark the request spanning the whole input as active, after which START-RESPOND changes the goal to RESPOND, allowing the actual response rules to fire.

```
Rule firings and wm changes:

166. START-DISPLAY-SET-RESPONSE
                   492 490 315 359
```

The display request is acted on by START-DISPLAY-SET-RESPONSE, which creates two goals, one to find actual objects that fit the description of the

```
=>wm:
493: (GOAL ^NAME TYPE-SEARCH
     ^STATUS ACTIVE ^SPEC T0078)
=>wm:
494: (GOAL ^NAME DISPLAY-SET
     ^STATUS ACTIVE ^TYPE 3 ^SPEC
     T0078)
```

```
Relevant wm elements previously
seen:


178: (SCHEMA-SPEC ^SET T0078 ^SLOT
     IS-A* ^FILLER TRUE_RIB ^STATE
     T0077 ^NUMBER SINGULAR)

165: (FACT ^ID T0074 ^SCHEMA
     TRUE_RIB ^SLOT INSTANCES
     ^FILLER RIB_NUMBER_7)
```

```
Rule firings and wm changes:


167. TYPE-SEARCH-START 493 359 165
=>wm:
495: (GOAL ^NAME DO-PCONCEPTG
     ^STATUS ACTIVE ^SPEC
     RIB_NUMBER_7)
=>wm:
496: (FACT ^ID T0094 ^SCHEMA
     RIB_NUMBER_7 ^SLOT IS-A*
     ^FILLER TRUE_RIB)

168. GIVE-FACT-NIL-SUPERSET 496
=>wm:
497: (SET ^TOKEN T0094)

169. PCONCEPTG-YES 495
=>wm:
498: (FACT ^ID T0095 ^SCHEMA
     RIB_NUMBER_7 ^SLOT IS-A
     ^FILLER TRUE_RIB)
```

set asked for, and the other to display these objects when found. The goals' set descriptor, T0078, in wm element 178, is the same set descriptor built by INDEFINITE-NP-REF-1 in rule firing number 32. It is shown again here for ease of reference.

The search for matching objects is carried out by loading into working memory the frames of instances of TRUE_RIB, and then recursively loading their instances, if necessary, until leaf frames are found, which are actual instances that should be displayed, rather than classes. This is started here by TYPE-SEARCH-START, which requests the loading of the frame for RIB_NUMBER_7, which is known to be an instance of TRUE_RIB because of the already-loaded FACT in element 165. This rule also creates a FACT indicating that the child frame IS-A* its parent, as a basis for generating the transitive closure of IS-A for any children of RIB_NUMBER_7, and also to serve as a common reference point for rules dealing with this frame.

The display rules expect every set they display to have set membership indicated. In order to make this work, GIVE-FACT-NIL-SUPERSET creates a SET element with no ^SUPERSET indicated.

```
<=wm:
495: (GOAL ^NAME DO-PCONCEPTG
      ^STATUS ACTIVE ^SPEC
      RIB_NUMBER_7)
```

Since there is no frame for RIB_NUMBER_7 in working memory yet, it is loaded. It just happens to consist of only one slot.

```
Rule firings:

170. DO-SINGULAR-DISPLAY


   RIB_NUMBER_7
   (IS-A (VALUE TRUE_RIB))
```

Since RIB_NUMBER_7 has no instances, it is a leaf, so the rule that does the actual display fires. In this case it is a rule to display a singleton set. It calls a Common Lisp function to print the frame, marks the goal of displaying satisfied, marks the main FACT for this frame as ^STATUS DISPLAYED to prevent accidental duplication in the case of plural sets, and creates a goal to indicate that the frame for RIB_NUMBER_7 is a member of the set T0078, the referent of the indefinite noun phase in the request. This is done via a goal mechanism to prevent duplication if this frame is already a member of this set.

```
171. MAKE-SET-YES
```

```
Set element created:

505: (SET ^TOKEN T0094 ^SUPERSET
     T0078)
```

Since this FACT was not a member of this set, MAKE-SET-YES creates an element indicating that it is. This allows future references to this set to correctly include the actual set members.

```
Rule firings:

172. REMOVE-REDUNDANT-NIL-SUPERSET
173. RESET-FACTS
174. FINISH-DISPLAY-SEARCH
```

Since there is now a real superset for this FACT, the next rule removes the null set membership indicator.

Since this display is over, RESET-FACTS changes the DISPLAYED status of the main FACT to CLEARED, so that it can be displayed if asked for again later. The next rule then removes the searching goal for similar reasons.

---

175. DISPLAY-SET-RESPONSE

Action and dialogue-relation elements:

77: (ACTION ^TOKEN A1 ^NEXT T0040
     ^UTT 0 ^STATE S1)
520: (ACTION ^TOKEN T0040 ^ACTION
     T0041 ^NEXT T0096 ^UTT 1
     ^PREV A1 ^STATE T0031)
521: (ACTION ^TOKEN T0096 ^ACTION
     T0090 ^UTT 2 ^PREV T0040
     ^STATE T0097)

512: (DIALOGUE-RELATION ^RELATION
     RESPONSE ^RELATOR T0096
     ^RELATEE T0040 ^UTT 2 ^STATE
     T0098)

Rule firings:

176. REQUEST-RESPONSE-ACTOR
177. DIALOGUE-SEG
178. END-OF-RESPONSE

DISPLAY-SET-RESPONSE records the fact that this response happened. This involves updating the representations of system and user actions, updating the word and utterance counters, creating a DIALOGUE-RELATION indicating that the display was a response to the user's utterance, and marking the request as satisfied. The ACTION elements shown here are the initial null action, the user's utterance, and the system's display action, respectively.

The next rule then records the system as being the actor in this request.

DIALOGUE-SEG records that this request/response pair forms a unit of dialogue.

Finally, END-OF-RESPONSE changes the goal from RESPOND to CASE-PARSE, to start the top-level cycle over again with the parser.

5.3. Functional verb phrase ellipsis

This sentence illustrates functional verb phrase ellipsis, since it is a lone noun phrase that refills a case from the preceding verb phrase. Its chart trace is shown in figure 5-3.

```
A     FLOATING
           RIB   *CR

!===! DETERMINER       T0113
!===! NOUN-PHRASE      T0115
      !===! NP-NULL       T0117
             !===! NOUN     T0118
      !========! NOUN       T0120
!=============! NOUN-PHRASE COMPLETE       T0125
!=============! NP-REF      T0126
!=============! VERB-PHRASE COMPLETE       T0128
!=============! ELLIPSIS       T0128
!-------------! VP-REF COMPLETE       T0129
!=============! VERB-PHRASE COMPLETE       T0131
!=============! ELLIPSIS       T0131
!-------------! VP-REF COMPLETE       T0132
!=============! VP-REF COMPLETE       T0132
             !===! PUNCTUATION       T0134
!=================! IMPERATIVE       T0135

Ready to assemble a meaning for state T0135

     RIB_NUMBER_12
        (IS-A (VALUE FLOATING_RIB))

             !===! DISPLAY       T0140
!=====================! RESPONSE       T0141
=====================! DIALOGUE-SEG       T0142
```

Figure 5-3:   Chart of second sentence in dialogue

Rule firings:

179. START-GOALS
180. GORO-PUSH-POSTED-GOAL-FIRST-
                      SUBGOAL
181. GORO-ACTIVATE-POSTED-TERMINAL-
                      GOAL

The initial goals are loaded into working memory, as for the first sentence, and the garbage collection goal, CP-CLEAN-UP, is selected and activated.

182. CLEAN-UP-UNCOND

   <A large number of firings of
   Clean-Up-Uncond, Clean-Up-Tree,
   and Clean-Up-Goals>

228. CLEAN-UP-UNCOND

This time, however, there is quite a bit of obsolete material in working memory, which is deleted by three rules: CLEAN-UP-UNCOND removes all elements that are used for temporary bookkeeping; CLEAN-UP-GOALS removes those goals that have a status of SUCCEEDED; and CLEAN-UP-TREE removes all the elements from states that did not get included in the final parse of the whole utterance. Although the old material that is deleted would not cause any incorrect actions, it does slow down the OPS5 matching process, and clutters up manual inspection of the working memory.

---

229. MESS-CLEANED-UP

Once all the garbage is deleted, MESS-CLEANED-UP fires, marking the goal as succeeded.

---

230. GORO-POP-AND-OR-AND*-SUCCESS
231. GORO-PUSH-SUBGOALED-GOAL-NEXT-
                      SUBGOAL
232. GORO-ACTIVATE-POSTED-TERMINAL-
                      GOAL
233. GET-INPUT

+ a floating rib

The goal selection and activation rules then activate the goal of getting the user's input, which again causes GET-INPUT to fire.

Input states:

609: (INPUT ^WORD A ^POSITION 9
     ^NEXT 10 ^UTT T ^PREV 8 ^END
     LEFT ^UTT-END LEFT ^STATE
     I0110)
610: (STATE ^STATUS POSTED ^UTT 3
     ^STATE I0110)
607: (INPUT ^WORD FLOATING
     ^POSITION 10 ^NEXT 11 ^UTT T
     ^PREV 9 ^STATE I0109)
608: (STATE ^STATUS POSTED ^UTT 3
     ^STATE I0109)
605: (INPUT ^WORD RIB ^POSITION 11
     ^NEXT 12 ^UTT T ^PREV 10
     ^STATE I0108)
606: (STATE ^STATUS POSTED ^UTT 3
     ^STATE I0108)
603: (INPUT ^WORD *CR ^POSITION 12
     ^NEXT 13 ^UTT T ^PREV 11 ^END
     RIGHT ^UTT-END RIGHT ^STATE
     I0107)
604: (STATE ^STATUS POSTED ^UTT 3
     ^STATE I0107)

600: (UTT-CNT ^UTT 3)
602: (WORD-CNT ^WORD 12)

These are the input states created from this user input, plus the utterance and word counters. The utterance counter is set to 3 because bookkeeping is simplified by counting the system's action of displaying the rib as "utterance" 2. Similarly, the word count is 12 because the display uses up one "word" location, as does the end-of-sentence punctuation *CR.

Rule firings:

234. GORO-POP-AND-OR-AND*-SUCCESS
235. GORO-PUSH-SUBGOALED-GOAL-NEXT-
                              SUBGOAL
236. GORO-ACTIVATE-POSTED-TERMINAL-
                                GOAL
237. START-UNDERSTAND
238. GET-FIRST-WORD
239. DICT-A
240. DET-NEW-NP

The goal for parsing the input is selected and activated, and the first word is activated by GET-FIRST-WORD.

This time the input starts with a noun phrase. Interpretation of the noun phrase begins as before, since this one also starts with a determiner. The determiner's definition state in working memory

241. AFTERMATH
242. NEXT-WORD
243. DICT-FLOATING_RIB-2-FLUSH1
244. AFTERMATH
245. NEXT-WORD
246. DICT-RIB-S
247. PCONCEPTG-NO

causes a new noun phrase to be started, and the first word of the idiomatic noun phrase *floating rib* causes a null state to be created. When *rib* is activated, the lexicon rule for the RIB frame again fires. The first real difference from the previous noun phrase is that, since the RIB frame is still in working memory from the last interpretation, PCONCEPTG-NO fires rather than PCONCEPTG-YES, so that no duplicate frame will be loaded.

---

248. DICT-FLOATING_RIB-2-S

"Floating rib" state:

658: (STATE ^STATUS POSTED ^UTT 3
      ^STATE T0120)
659: (ANCESTOR ^ANCESTOR I0109
      ^STATE T0120)
660: (ANCESTOR ^ANCESTOR I0108
      ^STATE T0120)
662: (POS ^CON T0121 ^TYPE NOUN
      ^STATE T0120 ^NUMBER SINGULAR
      ^OBJECT FLOATING_RIB)
663: (WORD-SEQ ^FIRST 10 ^LAST 11
      ^NEXT 12 ^PREV 9 ^STATE
      T0120)

This time the lexicon rule for *floating rib* fires, creating a definition similar to the one for *sternal rib* in the last sentence, except that the frame referred to this time is FLOATING_RIB.

Rule firings:

249. PCONCEPTG-YES

Since the FLOATING_RIB frame is not yet in working memory, PCONCEPTG-YES fires, loading it.

Floating_rib frame in wm:

664: (FACT ^ID T0122 ^SCHEMA
     FLOATING_RIB ^SLOT IS-A
     ^FILLER FALSE_RIB)
665: (FACT ^ID T0123 ^SCHEMA
     FLOATING_RIB ^SLOT INSTANCES
     ^FILLER RIB_NUMBER_11)
666: (FACT ^ID T0124 ^SCHEMA
     FLOATING_RIB ^SLOT INSTANCES
     ^FILLER RIB_NUMBER_12)

Rule firings:

250. NOUN-OLD-NP
251. INDEFINITE-NP-REF-1

Referent noun phrase state:

674: (STATE ^STATUS POSTED ^UTT 3
     ^STATE T0126)
675: (POS ^CON T0116 ^TYPE NP-REF
     ^STATE T0126)
676: (ANCESTOR ^ANCESTOR T0125
     ^STATE T0126)
677: (REFERENCE ^TOKEN T0116 ^DET
     INDEF ^HEAD FLOATING_RIB
     ^STATE T0126 ^NUMBER SINGULAR
     ^QUANT T ^DEREF T0127)
678: (SCHEMA-SPEC ^SET T0127 ^SLOT
     IS-A* ^FILLER FLOATING_RIB
     ^STATE T0126 ^NUMBER
     SINGULAR)
679: (WORD-SEQ ^FIRST 9 ^LAST 11
     ^NEXT 12 ^PREV 8 ^STATE
     T0126)

Once again, NOUN-OLD-NP creates a state representing a singular, indefinitely determined noun phrase, from which INDEFINITE-NP-REF-1 creates a SCHEMA-SPEC representing the set described, and indicates that this set is the referent of the noun phrase.

Rule firings:

252. ELLIPSIS-INITIAL-1-UNMARKED

Verb phrase state:

680: (STATE ^STATUS POSTED ^UTT 3
     ^STATE T0128)
681: (POS ^CON T0049 ^TYPE ELLIPSIS
     ^STATE T0128)
682: (POS ^CON T0049 ^STATUS
     COMPLETE ^TYPE VERB-PHRASE
     ^STATE T0128)
683: (ANCESTOR ^ANCESTOR T0092
     ^STATE T0128)
684: (ANCESTOR ^ANCESTOR T0125
     ^STATE T0128)
686: (ACT-REFERENCE ^TOKEN T0049
     ^ACTION DISPLAY ^MODE IMP
     ^STATE T0128 ^RECIP T0116
     ^OBJECT T0058 ^E-SUBJ T
     ^E-2ND T)
687: (CONSTRAINT ^ELEMENT T0049
     ^TYPE CASE ^SLOT RECIP
     ^FILLER T0116 ^STATE T0128)
688: (WORD-SEQ ^FIRST 9 ^LAST 11
     ^NEXT 12 ^PREV 8 ^STATE
     T0128)

Since a noun phrase at the left end of the input could be the start of an unmarked reformulation ellipsis, ELLIPSIS-INITIAL-1-UNMARKED fires. This rule, shown in chapter 4 in figures 4-18 and 4-19, takes the most recent verb phrase and creates a new verb phrase, in which this noun phrase replaces one of the old verb phrase's cases. It will fire once for each case that was filled in the preceding verb phrase. In this first firing, the recipient case is replaced, to produce the equivalent of *Display a sternal rib to a floating rib.*

Rule firings:

253. CONTINUE-OLD-VP-REF
254. CONSTRAINT-PROPAGATION

Verb phrase referent state:

689: (STATE ^STATUS PROPOSED ^UTT 3
     ^SPEC RECIP ^STATE T0129)

The existence of the resolved syntactic verb phrase, along with the referent for the antecedent verb phrase, allows CONTINUE-OLD-VP-REF, the intersentential version of the rule for continuing verb phrase references, to fire. It takes the ACT representing the referent of the antecedent and replaces the corresponding case with the referent

690: (POS ^CON T0049 ^STATUS
     COMPLETE ^TYPE VP-REF ^STATE
     T0129)
691: (ANCESTOR ^ANCESTOR T0128
     ^STATE T0129)
692: (ANCESTOR ^ANCESTOR T0089
     ^STATE T0129)
693: (ANCESTOR ^ANCESTOR T0126
     ^STATE T0129)
694: (ACT ^TOKEN T0130 ^ACTION
     DISPLAY ^MODE IMP ^ACTOR
     PSLI ^STATE T0129 ^RECIP
     T0127 ^OBJECT T0078
     ^E-SUBJ T)
695: (ACT-REFERENCE ^TOKEN T0049
     ^ACTION DISPLAY ^MODE IMP
     ^STATE T0129 ^RECIP T0116
     ^OBJECT T0058 ^DEREF T0130
     ^E-SUBJ T ^E-2ND T)
696: (WORD-SEQ ^FIRST 9 ^LAST 11
     ^NEXT 12 ^PREV 8 ^STATE
     T0129)
697: (CONSTRAINT ^ELEMENT T0049
     ^TYPE CASE ^SLOT RECIP
     ^FILLER T0116 ^STATE T0129)

of the new case filler. Since recipients must be people, the semantics checking rule will not fire on this state, and it will not get posted, but will just sit in the chart until deleted later by garbage collection rules.

Rule firings:

255. ELLIPSIS-INITIAL-1-UNMARKED
256. CONTINUE-OLD-VP-REF
257. CONSTRAINT-PROPAGATION
258. DISPLAY-OBJECT-CHECKER

Posted verb phrase referent state:

708: (POS ^CON T0049 ^STATUS
     COMPLETE ^TYPE VP-REF ^STATE
     T0132)
709: (ANCESTOR ^ANCESTOR T0131
     ^STATE T0132)

Since there is another filled case in the preceding verb phrase, ELLIPSIS-INITIAL-1-UNMARKED fires again, this time replacing the object case of the antecedent, to produce the equivalent of *Display a floating rib to Phil*.

This causes the elliptical verb phrase referent rule to build the corresponding proposed referent state (firing 256).

710: (ANCESTOR ^ANCESTOR T0089
       ^STATE T0132)
711: (ANCESTOR ^ANCESTOR T0126
       ^STATE T0132)
712: (ACT ^TOKEN T0133 ^ACTION
       DISPLAY ^MODE IMP ^ACTOR
       PSLI ^STATE T0132 ^RECIP
       PJH ^OBJECT T0127 ^E-SUBJ T)
713: (ACT-REFERENCE ^TOKEN T0049
       ^ACTION DISPLAY ^MODE IMP
       ^STATE T0132 ^RECIP T0086
       ^OBJECT T0116 ^DEREF T0133
       ^E-SUBJ T ^E-2ND T)
714: (WORD-SEQ ^FIRST 9 ^LAST 11
       ^NEXT 12 ^PREV 8 ^STATE
       T0132)
715: (CONSTRAINT ^ELEMENT T0049
       ^TYPE CASE ^SLOT OBJECT
       ^FILLER T0116 ^STATE T0132)
717: (STATE ^STATUS POSTED ^UTT 3
       ^STATE T0132)

Since this is an acceptable description of an action, the display object checking rule turns the proposed state into a posted state (firing 258), allowing other parsing rules to act on it.

Rule firings:

259. AFTERMATH
260. NEXT-WORD
261. DICT-PUNCT
262. REQUEST-SENTENCE

Request state:

726: (STATE ^STATUS POSTED ^UTT 3
       ^STATE T0135)
727: (POS ^CON T0136 ^TYPE
       IMPERATIVE ^STATE T0135)
728: (ANCESTOR ^ANCESTOR T0132
       ^STATE T0135)
729: (ANCESTOR ^ANCESTOR T0134
       ^STATE T0135)

The next word is the end of sentence punctuation mark *CR. This, following the posted imperative verb phrase built by the ellipsis rule, allows REQUEST-SENTENCE to fire, completing the construction of the new request.

```
730: (REQUEST ^TOKEN T0136 ^STATE
      T0135 ^OBJECT T0133)
731: (WORD-SEQ ^FIRST 9 ^LAST 12
      ^NEXT 13 ^PREV 8 ^STATE
      T0135)
```

Rule firings:

263. AFTERMATH
264. LAST-WORD
265. PARSING-FINISHED
266. GORO-POP-AND-OR-AND*-SUCCESS
267. GORO-PUSH-SUBGOALED-GOAL-NEXT-
                              SUBGOAL
268. GORO-ACTIVATE-POSTED-TERMINAL-
                              GOAL
269. FIND-FINAL-STATE-1
270. INSTALL-TOP-OBJECTS

     <A large number of firings
     of Install-Other-Objects
     and Install-Top-Objects>

317. INSTALL-TOP-OBJECTS
318. ASSEMBLY-DONE
319. GORO-POP-LAST-AND-OR-AND*-
                              SUCCESS
320. GORO-STOP-CLEANING-SUCCEEDED-
                              GOAL
321. PARSE-SUCCESS
322. ACTIVATE-REQUESTS
323. START-RESPOND
324. START-DISPLAY-SET-RESPONSE
325. TYPE-SEARCH-START
326. GIVE-FACT-NIL-SUPERSET
327. PCONCEPTG-YES
```

From this point on, things proceed exactly as in the previous sentence, except that FLOATING_RIB is the specified frame, so the FACTs loaded are different, one of which is displayed.

Also, REQUEST-RESPONSE-ACTOR does not fire this time after DISPLAY-SET-RESPONSE, because the actor case is already filled by *PSLI*, because it was filled from the antecedent verb phrase.

As we have seen, the interpretation of this type of elliptical phrase required only two special rules, one syntactic and one semantic, and the semantic rule is shared with other syntactic forms of functional reformulation ellipsis.
```

Relevant old wm elements:

678: (SCHEMA-SPEC ^SET T0127 ^SLOT
     IS-A* ^FILLER FLOATING_RIB
     ^STATE T0126 ^NUMBER
     SINGULAR)

666: (FACT ^ID T0124 ^SCHEMA
     FLOATING_RIB ^SLOT INSTANCES
     ^FILLER RIB_NUMBER_12)

Fact loaded:

863: (FACT ^ID T0138 ^SCHEMA
     RIB_NUMBER_12 ^SLOT IS-A
     ^FILLER FLOATING_RIB)

Rule firings:

328. DO-SINGULAR-DISPLAY

     RIB_NUMBER_12
         (IS-A (VALUE FLOATING_RIB))

329. MAKE-SET-YES
330. REMOVE-REDUNDANT-NIL-SUPERSET
331. RESET-FACTS
332. FINISH-DISPLAY-SEARCH
333. DISPLAY-SET-RESPONSE
334. DIALOGUE-SEG
335. END-OF-RESPONSE

5.4. Constituent verb phrase ellipsis

This sentence is a constituent ellipsis that illustrates syntactic ambiguity
being resolved through the influence of semantics. It is diagrammed in figure
5-4.

```
SHOW MARK *CR

!===! VERB-PHRASE 2      T0155
!===! VERB        T0155
!===! VERB-PHRASE 1      T0162
!===! VERB        T0162
!===! VP-REF 1        T0168
     !===! NOUN      T0170
     !===! PROPER-NOUN      T0170
     !===! NOUN-PHRASE COMPLETE       T0172
     !===! NP-REF      T0174
!========! VERB-PHRASE 1       T0175
!--------! VP-REF 1      T0176
!========! VP-REF 1      T0176
!========! VERB-PHRASE COMPLETE      T0178
!--------! VP-REF COMPLETE      T0179
           !===! PUNCTUATION      T0181
!========! VP-REF COMPLETE      T0182
!=============! IMPERATIVE      T0184

Ready to assemble a meaning for state T0184

     RIB_NUMBER_12
        (IS-A (VALUE FLOATING_RIB))

              !===! DISPLAY      T0187
!=================! RESPONSE      T0188
=================! DIALOGUE-SEG      T0189
```

Figure 5-4:   Chart of third sentence in dialogue

Rule firings:

336. START-GOALS
337. GORO-PUSH-POSTED-GOAL-FIRST-
                         SUBGOAL
338. GORO-ACTIVATE-POSTED-TERMINAL-
                         GOAL
339. CLEAN-UP-UNCOND

Once again, the initial goals are
loaded into working memory,
garbage collection is selected and
activated, and garbage is deleted
from working memory.

```
<A large number of firings of
 Clean-Up-Uncond, Clean-Up-Tree,
 and Clean-Up-Goals>
```

382. CLEAN-UP-UNCOND
383. MESS-CLEANED-UP

---

384. GORO-POP-AND-OR-AND*-SUCCESS

385. GORO-PUSH-SUBGOALED-GOAL-NEXT-
                                SUBGOAL
386. GORO-ACTIVATE-POSTED-TERMINAL-
                                  GOAL
387. GET-INPUT

+ show mark

Once again, after the garbage is cleaned up the user's utterance is read in.

Input states:

967: (INPUT ^WORD SHOW ^POSITION 14
      ^NEXT 15 ^UTT T ^PREV 13 ^END
      LEFT ^UTT-END LEFT ^STATE
      I0152)
968: (STATE ^STATUS POSTED ^UTT 5
      ^STATE I0152)
965: (INPUT ^WORD MARK ^POSITION 15
      ^NEXT 16 ^UTT T ^PREV 14
      ^STATE I0151)
966: (STATE ^STATUS POSTED ^UTT 5
      ^STATE I0151)
963: (INPUT ^WORD *CR ^POSITION 16
      ^NEXT 17 ^UTT T ^PREV 15 ^END
      RIGHT ^UTT-END RIGHT ^STATE
      I0150)
964: (STATE ^STATUS POSTED ^UTT 5
      ^STATE I0150)

960: (UTT-CNT ^UTT 5)
962: (WORD-CNT ^WORD 16)

Rule firings:

388. GORO-POP-AND-OR-AND*-SUCCESS
389. GORO-PUSH-SUBGOALED-GOAL-NEXT-
                              SUBGOAL
390. GORO-ACTIVATE-POSTED-TERMINAL-
                                GOAL
391. START-UNDERSTAND
392. GET-FIRST-WORD
393. DICT-SHOW
394. DICT-SHOW-IMP

"Show" state:

999: (STATE ^STATUS POSTED ~UTT 5
       ^STATE T0162)
1000: (ANCESTOR ^ANCESTOR I0152
       ^STATE T0162)
1001: (POS ^CON T0163 ^TYPE VERB
       ^STATE T0162)
1002: (POS ^CON T0163 ^STATUS 1
       ^TYPE VERB-PHRASE ^STATE
       T0162)
1003: (ACT-REFERENCE ^TOKEN T0163
       ^ACTION DISPLAY ^MODE IMP
       ^STATE T0162 ^E-SUBJ T)
1004: (EXPECT ^TOKEN T0164 ^CON
       T0163 ^TYPE E-MARKED ^SLOT
       BENE ^MARKER FOR ^STATE
       T0162)
1005: (EXPECT ^TOKEN T0165 ^CON
       T0163 ^TYPE E-UNMARKED ^SLOT
       OBJECT ^MARKER 2ND ^REQUIRED
       T ^STATE T0162)

As with the first utterance, this input begins with a verb, which causes two lexicon rules to load two definitions, one of which causes an imperative verb phrase referent to be started. While *show* has somewhat different surface cases from *display*, the action it refers to is the same type as in the first utterance.

1006: (EXPECT ^TOKEN T0166 ^CON
       T0163 ^TYPE E-MARKED ^SLOT
       RECIP ^MARKER TO ^STATE
       T0162)
1007: (EXPECT ^TOKEN T0167 ^CON
       T0163 ^TYPE E-UNMARKED ^SLOT
       RECIP ^MARKER 1ST ^STATE
       T0162)
1008: (WORD-SEQ ^FIRST 14 ^LAST 14
       ^NEXT 15 ^PREV 13 ^STATE
       T0162)

Rule firings:

395. IMPERATIVE-VERB-REF

Verb phrase referent state:

1009: (STATE ^STATUS POSTED ^UTT 5
       ^STATE T0168)
1010: (POS ^CON T0163 ^STATUS 1
       ^TYPE VP-REF ^STATE T0168)
1011: (ANCESTOR ^ANCESTOR T0162
       ^STATE T0168)
1012: (ACT ^TOKEN T0169 ^ACTION
       DISPLAY ^MODE IMP ^STATE
       T0168 ^E-SUBJ T)
1013: (ACT-REFERENCE ^TOKEN T0163
       ^ACTION DISPLAY ^MODE IMP
       ^STATE T0168 ^DEREF T0169
       ^E-SUBJ T)
1014: (WORD-SEQ ^FIRST 14 ^LAST 14
       ^NEXT 15 ^PREV 13 ^STATE
       T0168)

This is the start of the imperative verb referent for the imperative verb phrase.

Rule firings:

396. AFTERMATH
397. NEXT-WORD
398. DICT-NAME
399. NOUN-NEW-NP
400. DEREF-NAME

Referent noun phrase state:

1030: (STATE ^STATUS POSTED ^UTT 5
       ^STATE T0174)
1031: (POS ^CON T0173 ^TYPE NP-REF
       ^STATE T0174)
1032: (ANCESTOR ^ANCESTOR T0172
       ^STATE T0174)
1033: (REFERENCE ^TOKEN T0173 ^DET
       T ^HEAD MSF ^STATE T0174
       ^QUANT T ^DEREF MSF)
1034: (WORD-SEQ ^FIRST 15 ^LAST 15
       ^NEXT 16 ^PREV 14 ^STATE
       T0174)

Now the word *Mark* causes the lexicon rule for names to fire. Since there is a noun without a determiner or quantifier preceding it, NOUN-NEW-NP creates a new noun phrase for it. Then DEREF-NAME creates a state that indicates that this name refers to the person MSF.

Rule firings:

401. E-UNMARKED-1ST
402. PROPAGATE-UNREDUCED-VP
403. CONTINUE-VP-REF
404. CONSTRAINT-PROPAGATION
405. DISPLAY-RECIPIENT-CHECKER

Posted verb phrase referent state:

1047: (POS ^CON T0163 ^STATUS 1
       ^TYPE VP-REF ^STATE T0176)
1048: (ANCESTOR ^ANCESTOR T0175
       ^STATE T0176)
1049: (ANCESTOR ^ANCESTOR T0168
       ^STATE T0176)

In this utterance, because the verb *show* can have both a first object and a second object, the first unmarked noun phrase could fill either case. The first object is tried first.

The syntactic state created by E-UNMARKED-1ST has as many unfilled required cases as its predecessor verb phrase, since the first object is not required. So PROPAGATE-UNREDUCED-VP indicates that there is still one unfilled required case.

1050: (ANCESTOR ^ANCESTOR T0174
       ^STATE T0176)
1051: (ACT ^TOKEN T0177 ^ACTION
       DISPLAY ^MODE IMP ^STATE
       T0176 ^RECIP MSF ^E-SUBJ T)
1052: (ACT-REFERENCE ^TOKEN T0163
       ^ACTION DISPLAY ^MODE IMP
       ^STATE T0176 ^RECIP T0173
       ^DEREF T0177 ^E-SUBJ T)
1053: (WORD-SEQ ^FIRST 14 ^LAST 15
       ^NEXT 16 ^PREV 13 ^STATE
       T0176)
1054: (CONSTRAINT ^ELEMENT T0163
       ^TYPE CASE ^SLOT RECIP
       ^FILLER T0173 ^STATE T0176)
1056: (STATE ^STATUS POSTED ^UTT 5
       ^STATE T0176)
1052: (ACT-REFERENCE ^TOKEN T0163
       ^ACTION DISPLAY ^MODE IMP
       ^STATE T0176 ^RECIP T0173
       ^DEREF T0177 ^E-SUBJ T)
1053: (WORD-SEQ ^FIRST 14 ^LAST 15
       ^NEXT 16 ^PREV 13 ^STATE
       T0176)
1054: (CONSTRAINT ^ELEMENT T0163
       ^TYPE CASE ^SLOT RECIP
       ^FILLER T0173 ^STATE T0176)
1056: (STATE ^STATUS POSTED ^UTT 5
       ^STATE T0176)

The presence of the syntactic state, and a referent for its predecessor state, causes CONTINUE-VP-REF to build a referent state for the enlarged verb phrase. This state is only proposed, pending verification of its semantics.

The semantics checking rule for the recipient of a display action requires a known human being, so this state passes, and becomes posted, and available to the other parsing rules.

Rule firings:

406. E-UNMARKED-2ND
407. REDUCED-VP
408. DONE-VP
409. CONTINUE-VP-REF
410. CONSTRAINT-PROPAGATION

Now a verb phrase with *Mark* as the second object is built. Because the second object was a required case, REDUCED-VP indicates that the new verb phrase has one less unfilled required case. Since this leaves zero required cases, DONE-VP marks it as complete.

Proposed verb phrase referent
state:

1072: (STATE ^STATUS PROPOSED ^UTT
      5 ^SPEC OBJECT ^STATE T0179)
1073: (POS ^CON T0163 ^STATUS
      COMPLETE ^TYPE VP-REF ^STATE
      T0179)
1074: (ANCESTOR ^ANCESTOR T0178
      ^STATE T0179)
1075: (ANCESTOR ^ANCESTOR T0168
      ^STATE T0179)
1076: (ANCESTOR ^ANCESTOR T0174
      ^STATE T0179)
1077: (ACT ^TOKEN T0180 ^ACTION
      DISPLAY ^MODE IMP ^STATE
      T0179 ^OBJECT MSF ^E-SUBJ T)
1078: (ACT-REFERENCE ^TOKEN T0163
      ^ACTION DISPLAY ^MODE IMP
      ^STATE T0179 ^OBJECT T0173
      ^DEREF T0180 ^E-SUBJ T
      ^E-2ND T)
1079: (WORD-SEQ ^FIRST 14 ^LAST 15
      ^NEXT 16 ^PREV 13 ^STATE
      T0179)
1080: (CONSTRAINT ^ELEMENT T0163
      ^TYPE CASE ^SLOT OBJECT
      ^FILLER T0173 ^STATE T0179)

Rule firings:

411. AFTERMATH
412. NEXT-WORD
413. DICT-PUNCT
414. REQUEST-ELLIPSIS
415. REDUCED-VP
416. DONE-VP

A referent verb phrase state is then built. Since the object of a display must be a known database object, the semantics checking rule does not fire, and the referent state remains proposed. The semantic failure of this state resolves the potential case role ambiguity of this utterance, since this state does not become available to the other parsing rules.

Here the verb phrase constituent reformulation ellipsis rule fires, once the end-of-sentence punctuation is activated. This happens because there is a verb phrase referent that extends from the beginning of the input to the punctuation mark that

---

Referent verb phrase state:

1089: (STATE ^STATUS POSTED ^UTT 5
       ^STATE T0182)
1091: (ANCESTOR ^ANCESTOR T0132
       ^STATE T0182)
1092: (ANCESTOR ^ANCESTOR T0176
       ^STATE T0182)
1093: (ACT ^TOKEN T0183 ^ACTION
       DISPLAY ^MODE IMP ^STATE
       T0182 ^RECIP MSF ^OBJECT
       T0127 ^E-SUBJ T)
1094: (ACT-REFERENCE ^TOKEN T0163
       ^ACTION DISPLAY ^MODE IMP
       ^STATE T0182 ^RECIP T0173
       ^OBJECT T0116 ^DEREF T0183
       ^E-SUBJ T)
1095: (CONSTRAINT ^ELEMENT T0163
       ^TYPE CASE ^SLOT OBJECT
       ^FILLER T0116 ^STATE T0182)
1103: (POS ^CON T0163 ^STATUS
       COMPLETE ^TYPE VP-REF ^STATE
       T0182)
1105: (WORD-SEQ ^FIRST 14 ^LAST 15
       ^NEXT 16 ^PREV 13 ^STATE
       T0182)

has an unfilled required case, and this case can be filled from an antecedent utterance. So the object of this action (in element 1093) becomes set T0127, which is identically the set displayed in the last system display action (page 130).

Rule firings:

417. REQUEST-SENTENCE
418. CONSTRAINT-PROPAGATION
419. AFTERMATH
420. LAST-WORD
421. PARSING-FINISHED
422. GORO-POP-AND-OR-AND*-SUCCESS
423. GORO-PUSH-SUBGOALED-GOAL-NEXT-
                          SUBGOAL

From this point, things proceed as in the other utterances, until the display action starts. Then, because the object to be displayed is a set that has already been made explicit, no searching, loading, or creation of null supersets is necessary between the firing of START-DISPLAY-SET-RESPONSE and the actual display by DO-SINGULAR-DISPLAY.

```
424. GORO-ACTIVATE-POSTED-TERMINAL-
                                 GOAL
425. FIND-FINAL-STATE-1
426. INSTALL-TOP-OBJECTS

    <A large number of firings
     of Install-Other-Objects
     and Install-Top-Objects>

484. INSTALL-TOP-OBJECTS
485. ASSEMBLY-DONE
486. GORO-POP-LAST-AND-OR-AND*-
                              SUCCESS
487. GORO-STOP-CLEANING-SUCCEEDED-
                                 GOAL
488. PARSE-SUCCESS
489. ACTIVATE-REQUESTS
490. START-RESPOND
491. START-DISPLAY-SET-RESPONSE
492. DO-SINGULAR-DISPLAY

    RIB_NUMBER_12
        (IS-A (VALUE FLOATING_RIB))

493. MAKE-SET-NO
494. RESET-FACTS
495. FINISH-DISPLAY-SEARCH
496. DISPLAY-SET-RESPONSE
497. REQUEST-RESPONSE-ACTOR
498. DIALOGUE-SEG
499. END-OF-RESPONSE
```

After the display, MAKE-SET-NO fires, deleting the goal to mark set membership, since the set membership of this frame is already recorded. There is no null superset to remove, so RESET-FACTS fires next, making this fact available for future display actions. Notice that this production's action last time made it possible for this frame to be displayed this time.

The last noteworthy difference is that because this is a new verb phrase, REQUEST-RESPONSE-ACTOR is needed to indicate that *PSLI* was the actor in this action.

5.5. Another functional verb phrase ellipsis

This sentence has two new features: it includes two cases which fit into the antecedent verb phrase, and uses the "other" form of reference to indicate that the user wishes to see a set disjoint from the previous ones. Its chart is shown in figure 5-5.

```
ANOTHER
        TRUE RIB  TO    ME    *CR

!===! NP-SPECIAL      T0205
!===! NOUN-PHRASE       T0207
      !===! NP-NULL      T0209
            !===! NOUN      T0210
            !========! NOUN      T0212
!=============! NOUN-PHRASE COMPLETE       T0214
!=============! NP-REF      T0215
!=============! VERB-PHRASE COMPLETE       T0229
!=============! ELLIPSIS      T0229
!-------------! VP-REF COMPLETE      T0230
!=============! VERB-PHRASE COMPLETE       T0232
!=============! ELLIPSIS      T0232
!-------------! VP-REF COMPLETE      T0233
!=============! VP-REF COMPLETE      T0233
                !===! PREPOSITION      T0235
                    !===! NOUN      T0236
                    !===! PRONOUN      T0236
                    !===! NOUN-PHRASE COMPLETE       T0238
                    !===! NP-REF      T0240
!======================! VERB-PHRASE COMPLETE      T0241
!======================! ELLIPSIS      T0241
!----------------------! VP-REF COMPLETE      T0242
!======================! VP-REF COMPLETE      T0242
                    !===! PUNCTUATION      T0244
!===========================! IMPERATIVE      T0245

Ready to assemble a meaning for state T0245

    RIB_NUMBER_1
      (IS-A (VALUE TRUE_RIB))

                        !===! DISPLAY      T0248
!=================================! RESPONSE      T0249
==================================! DIALOGUE-SEG      T0250
```

Figure 5-5:   Chart of fourth sentence in dialogue

```
Rule firings:

500. START-GOALS
501. GORO-PUSH-POSTED-GOAL-FIRST-
                          SUBGOAL
502. GORO-ACTIVATE-POSTED-TERMINAL-
                          GOAL
503. CLEAN-UP-UNCOND

   <A large number of firings of
   Clean-Up-Uncond, Clean-Up-Tree,
   and Clean-Up-Goals>

547. CLEAN-UP-UNCOND
548. MESS-CLEANED-UP
```

Once again, the initial goals are loaded into working memory, garbage collection is selected and activated, and garbage is deleted from working memory.

```
549. GORO-POP-AND-OR-AND*-SUCCESS
550. GORO-PUSH-SUBGOALED-GOAL-NEXT-
                          SUBGOAL
551. GORO-ACTIVATE-POSTED-TERMINAL-
                          GOAL
552. GET-INPUT

+ another sternal rib to me
```

Once again, after the garbage is cleaned up the user's utterance is read in.

```
Input states:

1372: (INPUT ^WORD ANOTHER
         ^POSITION 18 ^NEXT 19 ^UTT T
         ^PREV 17 ^END LEFT ^UTT-END
         LEFT ^STATE I0202)
1373: (STATE ^STATUS POSTED ^UTT 7
         ^STATE I0202)
1370: (INPUT ^WORD STERNAL
         ^POSITION 19 ^NEXT 20 ^UTT T
         ^PREV 18 ^STATE I0201)
1371: (STATE ^STATUS POSTED ^UTT 7
         ^STATE I0201)
```

```
1368: (INPUT ^WORD RIB ^POSITION 20
       ^NEXT 21 ^UTT T ^PREV 19
       ^STATE I0200)
1369: (STATE ^STATUS POSTED ^UTT 7
       ^STATE I0200)
1366: (INPUT ^WORD TO ^POSITION 21
       ^NEXT 22 ^UTT T ^PREV 20
       ^STATE I0199)
1367: (STATE ^STATUS POSTED ^UTT 7
       ^STATE I0199)
1364: (INPUT ^WORD ME ^POSITION 22
       ^NEXT 23 ^UTT T ^PREV 21
       ^STATE I0198)
1365: (STATE ^STATUS POSTED ^UTT 7
       ^STATE I0198)
1362: (INPUT ^WORD *CR ^POSITION 23
       ^NEXT 24 ^UTT T ^PREV 22
       ^END RIGHT ^UTT-END RIGHT
       ^STATE I0197)
1363: (STATE ^STATUS POSTED ^UTT 7
       ^STATE I0197)

1359: (UTT-CNT ^UTT 7)
1361: (WORD-CNT ^WORD 23)
```

```
Rule firings:

553. GORO-POP-AND-OR-AND*-SUCCESS
554. GORO-PUSH-SUBGOALED-GOAL-NEXT-
                              SUBGOAL
555. GORO-ACTIVATE-POSTED-TERMINAL-
                                 GOAL
556. START-UNDERSTAND
557. GET-FIRST-WORD
558. DICT-ANOTHER
```

This time the first word is *another*. This word has its own syntactic class, since it is a combination of a determiner and an "other" class word.

"Another" state:

1393: (STATE ^STATUS POSTED ^UTT 7
       ^STATE T0205)
1394: (ANCESTOR ^ANCESTOR I0202
       ^STATE T0205)
1395: (POS ^CON T0206 ^TYPE
       NP-SPECIAL ^STATE T0205
       ^OBJECT ANOTHER)
1396: (WORD-SEQ ^FIRST 18 ^LAST 18
       ^NEXT 19 ^PREV 17 ^STATE
       T0205)

Rule firings:

559. ANOTHER-NEW-NP

Noun phrase state:

1397: (STATE ^STATUS POSTED ^UTT 7
       ^STATE T0207)
1398: (ANCESTOR ^ANCESTOR T0205
       ^STATE T0207)
1399: (POS ^CON T0208 ^TYPE
       NOUN-PHRASE ^STATE T0207)
1400: (REFERENCE ^TOKEN T0208 ^DET
       INDEF ^OTHER T ^STATE T0207
       ^QUANT T)
1401: (WORD-SEQ ^FIRST 18 ^LAST 18
       ^NEXT 19 ^PREV 17 ^STATE
       T0207)

Rule firings:

560. AFTERMATH
561. NEXT-WORD
562. DICT-TRUE_RIB-2-FLUSH1
563. AFTERMATH
564. NEXT-WORD

There is a special rule for starting a noun phrase with *another*, which marks the new noun phrase as both indefinitely determined and ^OTHER T. This is a semantic marker, indicating that this set needs to be disjoint from any similar ones currently in working memory. Since quantifiers should not occur in this noun phrase after this word, ^QUANT is set to T.

The usual train of events occurs, with PCONCEPTG-NO firing twice, since both RIB and TRUE_RIB frames are still in working memory. When INDEFINITE-NP-REF-1 creates the indefinite set description, the ^OTHER T attribute is included.

565. DICT-RIB-S
566. PCONCEPTG-NO
567. DICT-TRUE_RIB-2-S
568. PCONCEPTG-NO
569. NOUN-OLD-NP
570. INDEFINITE-NP-REF-1

Referent noun phrase state:

1433: (STATE ^STATUS POSTED ^UTT 7
        ^STATE T0215)
1434: (POS ^CON T0208 ^TYPE NP-REF
        ^STATE T0215)
1435: (ANCESTOR ^ANCESTOR T0214
        ^STATE T0215)
1436: (REFERENCE ^TOKEN T0208 ^DET
        INDEF ^OTHER T ^HEAD
        TRUE_RIB ^STATE T0215
        ^NUMBER SINGULAR ^QUANT T
        ^DEREF T0216)
1437: (SCHEMA-SPEC ^SET T0216 ^SLOT
        IS-A* ^FILLER TRUE_RIB
        ^STATE T0215 ^NUMBER
        SINGULAR)
1438: (WORD-SEQ ^FIRST 18 ^LAST 20
        ^NEXT 21 ^PREV 17 ^STATE
        T0215)

Rule firings and wm changes:

571. START-OTHER-NP-REF
                    1436 1437 1433
=>wm:
1439: (SCHEMA-SPEC ^SET T0216 ^SLOT
        *OTHER-THAN ^STATE T0215)
=>wm:
1440: (GOAL ^NAME TYPE-SEARCH
        ^STATUS ACTIVE ^SPEC T0216)

The existence of a referent noun phrase state with an "other" semantic marker causes START-OTHER-NP-REF to fire, starting a search for any preceding sets that this set should be "other" than, that is, any sets matching the rest of its specification.

```
572. OTHER-NP-REF 1440 1439 1437
                  1433 359 505 509 509
<=wm:
1440: (GOAL ^NAME TYPE-SEARCH
      ^STATUS ACTIVE ^SPEC T0216)
=>wm:
1442: (GOAL ^NAME TYPE-SEARCH
      ^STATUS SUSPENDED ^SPEC
      T0216)
=>wm:
1443: (SCHEMA-SPEC ^SET T0216 ^SLOT
      *OTHER-THAN ^FILLER T0078
      ^STATE T0215)
```

This immediately succeeds, since set T0078, created by the user's first utterance (see page 113), is a TRUE_RIB. The *OTHER-THAN constraint relationship is recorded, and the searching goal is suspended, so that if there are no other candidate references, no more time will be spent searching.

```
Current set data structures:

359: (SCHEMA-SPEC ^SET T0078 ^UTT 1
     ^SLOT IS-A* ^FILLER TRUE_RIB
     ^STATE T0077 ^NUMBER
     SINGULAR)
505: (SET ^TOKEN T0094 ^SUPERSET
     T0078)
509: (FACT ^ID T0094 ^STATUS
     CLEARED ^SCHEMA RIB_NUMBER_7
     ^SLOT IS-A* ^FILLER TRUE_RIB)

778: (SCHEMA-SPEC ^SET T0127 ^UTT 3
     ^SLOT IS-A* ^FILLER
     FLOATING_RIB ^STATE T0126
     ^NUMBER SINGULAR)
870: (SET ^TOKEN T0137 ^SUPERSET
     T0127)
1270: (FACT ^ID T0137 ^STATUS
      CLEARED ^SCHEMA
      RIB_NUMBER_12 ^SLOT IS-A*
      ^FILLER FLOATING_RIB)
```

```
1437:  (SCHEMA-SPEC ^SET T0216 ^SLOT
        IS-A* ^FILLER TRUE_RIB
        ^STATE T0215 ^NUMBER
        SINGULAR)
1439:  (SCHEMA-SPEC ^SET T0216 ^SLOT
        *OTHER-THAN ^STATE T0215)
1443:  (SCHEMA-SPEC ^SET T0216 ^SLOT
        *OTHER-THAN ^FILLER T0078
        ^STATE T0215)
```

Rule firings and wm changes:

573. OTHER-NP-REF-KEEP-GOING
                1442 1439 1437 1433 778
<=wm:
1442: (GOAL ^NAME TYPE-SEARCH
        ^STATUS SUSPENDED ^SPEC
        T0216)
=>wm:
1445: (GOAL ^NAME TYPE-SEARCH
        ^STATUS ACTIVE ^SPEC T0216)

Rule firings:

574. TYPE-SEARCH-START
575. GIVE-FACT-NIL-SUPERSET
576. PCONCEPTG-YES
577. TYPE-SEARCH-START
578. GIVE-FACT-NIL-SUPERSET
579. PCONCEPTG-YES
580. TYPE-SEARCH-START
581. GIVE-FACT-NIL-SUPERSET
582. PCONCEPTG-YES
583. TYPE-SEARCH-START
584. GIVE-FACT-NIL-SUPERSET
585. PCONCEPTG-YES
586. TYPE-SEARCH-START
587. GIVE-FACT-NIL-SUPERSET

Since other sets exist, which could conceivably be TRUE_RIBs by a longer chain of IS-A relations, OTHER-NP-REF-KEEP-GOING restarts the search goal, to find out whether they really should be disjoint from this set.

This causes the elaboration of each TRUE_RIB type frame currently in working memory, none of which have any descendants. So the other sets in working memory are not TRUE_RIBs, END-FULL-SEARCH terminates the search, and we are left with the single constraint that this set be disjoint from T0078.

588. PCONCEPTG-YES
589. TYPE-SEARCH-START
590. GIVE-FACT-NIL-SUPERSET
591. PCONCEPTG-YES
592. END-FULL-SEARCH

---

593. ELLIPSIS-INITIAL-1-UNMARKED
594. CONTINUE-OLD-VP-REF
595. CONSTRAINT-PROPAGATION

Proposed referent verb phrase
state:

1487: (STATE ^STATUS PROPOSED ^UTT
       7 ^SPEC RECIP ^STATE T0230)
1488: (POS ^CON T0163 ^STATUS
       COMPLETE ^TYPE VP-REF ^STATE
       T0230)
1489: (ANCESTOR ^ANCESTOR T0229
       ^STATE T0230)
1490: (ANCESTOR ^ANCESTOR T0182
       ^STATE T0230)
1491: (ANCESTOR ^ANCESTOR T0215
       ^STATE T0230)
1492: (ACT ^TOKEN T0231 ^ACTION
       DISPLAY ^MODE IMP ^ACTOR
       PSLI ^STATE T0230 ^RECIP
       T0216 ^OBJECT T0127 ^E-SUBJ
       T)
1493: (ACT-REFERENCE ^TOKEN T0163
       ^ACTION DISPLAY ^MODE IMP
       ^STATE T0230 ^RECIP T0208
       ^OBJECT T0116 ^DEREF T0231
       ^E-SUBJ T)
1494: (WORD-SEQ ^FIRST 18 ^LAST 20
       ^NEXT 21 ^PREV 17 ^STATE
       T0230)

As before, there are two cases in the antecedent utterance, so two syntactic ellipsis instantiations are created, each of which generates a semantic referent description. Only the one that is semantically acceptable is posted for further action.

This is the one that failed its semantic check.

```
1495: (CONSTRAINT ^ELEMENT T0163
      ^TYPE CASE ^SLOT RECIP
      ^FILLER T0208 ^STATE T0230)
```

Rule firings:

596. ELLIPSIS-INITIAL-1-UNMARKED
597. CONTINUE-OLD-VP-REF
598. CONSTRAINT-PROPAGATION
599. DISPLAY-OBJECT-CHECKER

This is the second ellipsis instantiation referent, which passed its semantic check to become posted.

Posted referent verb phrase state:

```
1506: (POS ^CON T0163 ^STATUS
      COMPLETE ^TYPE VP-REF ^STATE
      T0233)
1507: (ANCESTOR ^ANCESTOR T0232
      ^STATE T0233)
1508: (ANCESTOR ^ANCESTOR T0182
      ^STATE T0233)
1509: (ANCESTOR ^ANCESTOR T0215
      ^STATE T0233)
1510: (ACT ^TOKEN T0234 ^ACTION
      DISPLAY ^MODE IMP ^ACTOR
      *PSLI* ^STATE T0233 ^RECIP
      MSF ^OBJECT T0215 ^E-SUBJ T)
1511: (ACT-REFERENCE ^TOKEN T0163
      ^ACTION DISPLAY ^MODE IMP
      ^STATE T0233 ^RECIP T0173
      ^OBJECT T0208 ^DEREF T0234
      ^E-SUBJ T)
1512: (WORD-SEQ ^FIRST 18 ^LAST 20
      ^NEXT 21 ^PREV 17 ^STATE
      T0233)
1513: (CONSTRAINT ^ELEMENT T0163
      ^TYPE CASE ^SLOT OBJECT
      ^FILLER T0208 ^STATE T0233)
1515: (STATE ^STATUS POSTED ^UTT 7
      ^STATE T0233)
```

Rule firings:

600. AFTERMATH
601. NEXT-WORD
602. DICT-PREP
603. AFTERMATH
604. NEXT-WORD
605. DICT-ME
606. NOUN-NEW-NP
607. DEREF-ME

The system moves on to read *to* and *me*. *Me* has its own referent-finding rule, which checks to see who the current user is, and indicates that person as the referent.

Referent noun phrase state:

1539: (STATE ^STATUS POSTED ^UTT 7
        ^STATE T0240)
1540: (POS ^CON T0239 ^TYPE NP-REF
        ^STATE T0240)
1541: (ANCESTOR ^ANCESTOR T0238
        ^STATE T0240)
1542: (REFERENCE ^TOKEN T0239 ^DET
        T ^HEAD *ME* ^STATE T0240
        ^QUANT T ^DEREF REF)
1543: (WORD-SEQ ^FIRST 22 ^LAST 22
        ^NEXT 23 ^PREV 21 ^STATE
        T0240)

Rule firings:

608. ELLIPSIS-MARKED
609. CONSTRAINT-PROPAGATION
610. CONTINUE-VP-REF
611. CONSTRAINT-PROPAGATION
612. CONSTRAINT-PROPAGATION
613. DISPLAY-RECIPIENT-CHECKER

An ellipsis rule fires that adds a marked case onto an elliptical verb phrase. It is similar to the corresponding full sentence E-MARKED in the first example, on page 116, except that it uses the expectations defined in the antecedent.

Then the usual rule for continuing a verb phrase referent fires, since the system is extending a verb phrase within one utterance. The resulting state is approved by the semantics checking rule, making it available to the other parsing rules.

Referent verb phrase state:

1556: (POS ^CON T0163 ^STATUS
      COMPLETE ^TYPE VP-REF ^STATE
      T0242)
1557: (ANCESTOR ^ANCESTOR T0241
      ^STATE T0242)
1558: (ANCESTOR ^ANCESTOR T0233
      ^STATE T0242)
1559: (ANCESTOR ^ANCESTOR T0240
      ^STATE T0242)
1560: (ACT ^TOKEN T0243 ^ACTION
      DISPLAY ^MODE IMP ^ACTOR
      PSLI ^STATE T0242 ^RECIP
      REF ^OBJECT T0216 ^E-SUBJ T)
1561: (ACT-REFERENCE ^TOKEN T0163
      ^ACTION DISPLAY ^MODE IMP
      ^STATE T0242 ^RECIP T0239
      ^OBJECT T0208 ^DEREF T0243
      ^E-SUBJ T)
1562: (WORD-SEQ ^FIRST 18 ^LAST 22
      ^NEXT 23 ^PREV 17 ^STATE
      T0242)
1563: (CONSTRAINT ^ELEMENT T0163
      ^TYPE CASE ^SLOT OBJECT
      ^FILLER T0208 ^STATE T0242)
1564: (CONSTRAINT ^ELEMENT T0163
      ^TYPE CASE ^SLOT RECIP
      ^FILLER T0239 ^STATE T0242)
1566: (STATE ^STATUS POSTED ^UTT 7
      ^STATE T0242)

Rule firings:

614. AFTERMATH
615. NEXT-WORD
616. DICT-PUNCT
617. REQUEST-SENTENCE
618. AFTERMATH

Once again, things proceed as usual. As in the previous utterance, no rules fire between START-DISPLAY-SET-RESPONSE and DO-SINGULAR-DISPLAY because all the necessary set membership information is already in place, this

```
619. LAST-WORD
620. PARSING-FINISHED
621. GORO-POP-AND-OR-AND*-SUCCESS
622. GORO-PUSH-SUBGOALED-GOAL-NEXT-
                            SUBGOAL
623. GORO-ACTIVATE-POSTED-TERMINAL-
                               GOAL
624. FIND-FINAL-STATE-1
625. INSTALL-TOP-OBJECTS

     <A large number of firings
      of Install-Other-Objects
      and Install-Top-Objects>

709. INSTALL-TOP-OBJECTS
710. ASSEMBLY-DONE
711. GORO-POP-LAST-AND-OR-AND*-
                            SUCCESS
712. GORO-STOP-CLEANING-SUCCEEDED-
                               GOAL
713. PARSE-SUCCESS
714. ACTIVATE-REQUESTS
715. START-RESPOND
716. START-DISPLAY-SET-RESPONSE
717. DO-SINGULAR-DISPLAY

     RIB_NUMBER_1
        (IS-A (VALUE TRUE_RIB))

718. MAKE-SET-YES
719. REMOVE-REDUNDANT-NIL-SUPERSET
```

time due to the search for any "other" sets.

After the display, MAKE-SET-YES fires, because this particular fact has not been displayed before, so its membership in the set displayed by this action is recorded.

```
Set data structures:

359: (SCHEMA-SPEC ^SET T0078 ^UTT 1
      ^SLOT IS-A* ^FILLER TRUE_RIB
      ^STATE T0077 ^NUMBER
      SINGULAR)
505: (SET ^TOKEN T0094 ^SUPERSET
      T0078)
```

Here we present in one place all the set membership information in working memory for objects displayed during this interaction.

509: (FACT ^ID T0094 ^STATUS
     CLEARED ^SCHEMA RIB_NUMBER_7
     ^SLOT IS-A* ^FILLER TRUE_RIB)
778: (SCHEMA-SPEC ^SET T0127 ^UTT 3
     ^SLOT IS-A* ^FILLER
     FLOATING_RIB ^STATE T0126
     ^NUMBER SINGULAR)
870: (SET ^TOKEN T0137 ^SUPERSET
     T0127)
1270: (FACT ^ID T0137 ^STATUS
      CLEARED ^SCHEMA
      RIB_NUMBER_12 ^SLOT IS-A*
      ^FILLER FLOATING_RIB)

1671: (SCHEMA-SPEC ^SET T0216 ^UTT
      7 ^SLOT IS-A* ^FILLER
      TRUE_RIB ^STATE T0215
      ^NUMBER SINGULAR)
1667: (SCHEMA-SPEC ^SET T0216 ^UTT
      7 ^SLOT *OTHER-THAN ^STATE
      T0215)
1665: (SCHEMA-SPEC ^SET T0216 ^UTT
      7 ^SLOT *OTHER-THAN ^FILLER
      T0078 ^STATE T0215)
1788: (SET ^TOKEN T0227 ^SUPERSET
      T0216)
1786: (FACT ^ID T0227 ^STATUS
      DISPLAYED ^SCHEMA
      RIB_NUMBER_1 ^SLOT IS-A*
      ^FILLER TRUE_RIB)

Rule firings:

720. RESET-FACTS
721. FINISH-DISPLAY-SEARCH
722. DISPLAY-SET-RESPONSE
723. DIALOGUE-SEG
724. END-OF-RESPONSE

5.6. Conclusion

We have seen here how rules operating within the production system framework can simply and naturally refer to objects currently residing in working memory, whether in current or previous utterances. This achieves a level of practical dialogue cohesion uncommon in natural language systems. A number of specific observations can be made concerning the implementation of this system.

The use of OPS5 as the system's programming language has both good and bad points. The main positive feature was the style of programming encouraged by the production system architecture that OPS5 embodies. Data structures in working memory are accessed by pattern matching; program control is achieved through the creation and manipulation of declarative goals; complex data structures are connected through matching identification tokens. Programming in such a system seems to lead naturally to intuitively pleasing solutions: the most elegant way to implement a function tends to also be the most intuitively plausible.

The primary objective advantage of the use of OPS5 is the broad-band access to data structures representing previous utterances that the use of working memory encourages. It is fairly straightforward to produce the intersentential versions of rules that act within sentences, once the decision is made as to what the desired behavior is. It is our belief that the future development of natural language processing systems will show a tendency to lose the barrier between individual utterances, in favor of broad communication between processed utterances, just as systems developed so far have tended over time to drop the barriers between lexical, syntactic, and semantic modules in favor of broad communication between different knowledge sources.

Since we were not attempting to build a real-time system, speed is not a major issue. OPS5 is fast enough for development work, and there are faster production system languages available that might reach real-time speed, if desired, such as OPS83. The main disadvantage of using OPS5 is the low level programming required. The use of matching unique tokens in working memory elements is a powerful programming technique, allowing the construction of sets and doubly-linked lists of elements as well as simple pointers. But these tokens must be generated and matched explicitly in the rules that the programmer writes. There is a clear need for something like an "OPS5 compiler", which would allow the user to specify set membership, links, and other structures, both in matching and creating, without having to explicitly manipulate gensyms. One could conceive of carrying this further, and having language constructs that would compile into sets of rules and goals controlling their activation. Similarly, there is a need for better debugging tools, operating at a higher level than the current ones. The Knowledge Craft^{TM} system, among others, has made some progress along these lines [Knowledge 86].

The main reason for using charts in this system is the elegant way in which they handle ambiguity, and the natural way they fit into the production system framework when used for both the syntax and semantics of the representation of an utterance. Data structures that were tried previously seem quite awkward and needlessly complicated in comparison. In terms of dialogue phenomena, the main advantage of the chart representation, in addition to its tolerance of the initial ambiguity in ellipsis resolution, is its ability to represent multiple-sentence charts, as discussed in the preceding chapter. Ambiguous utterances that can be resolved based on the interpretations of other utterances are easily handled using the chart representation.

In addition to these specific implementation properties, more general characteristics can be observed. The modularity of the system as implemented varies, with some functions well modularized, while others could be improved. The loading of frames, manipulation of goals and sets, and searches of the semantic network are all implemented in a fairly modular fashion, through the use of sets of rules activated by goals. The lexicon is made modular in a different fashion, by having lexicon frames that are converted into several OPS5 rules each at load time through the action of what are essentially OPS5 macros. The recording of the system's own actions, described in detail in chapter 6 below, and the action of the display routines are examples of functions that should be reworked into a more modular, extensible form.

One area in which modularization could be very useful is in the creation of ellipsis meta-rules. In the current system, an intersentential version of each syntactic rule needs to be created, if the syntactic form handled by the rule is to take part in reformulation ellipsis. As the number of syntactic forms handled increases, this becomes more of a problem. It should be possible to make this more modular, either by breaking up the action of each current rule into several rules, or by creating larger-scale constructs, similar to the lexicon frames now used. Even without this improvement, the system is not terribly hard to extend, since the additional ellipsis rule is generally a fairly direct modification of the corresponding syntactic rule.

A possible source of concern is the lack of any "forgetting" ability in this system. Except for the deletion of incorrect chart states, information simply accumulates in working memory as the system runs. Nothing was done about this because we see no clear criterion for the end of a context space in this domain that could signal that the old context should be forgotten. Although the system never runs long enough for memory size to be a problem, the matching time of OPS5 systems depends on the size of working memory. This was originally a problem in this system, since the matching time for the parsing rules was highly dependent on the total amount of input in working memory. The rules were rewritten using advice from Brownston et al. [Brownston 85] so that this is no longer the case; the system slows down slightly for long dialogues, but not enough to cause a problem.

The next chapter presents some more general conclusions about this work.

Chapter 6
Conclusion

6.1. Contributions

We have developed and implemented an integrated computational method for understanding natural language. Within this scheme, we have developed and implemented an integrated set of techniques for ellipsis resolution, comprehension of multiple sentence utterances, natural language generation, noun phrase reference resolution, knowledge base access, and error detection and correction. We have also developed an analytical taxonomy of intersentential ellipsis, based on the types of processing necessary to interpret these ellipses.

This integrated computational method consists of an extension of chart parsing to include incremental semantics, adapted to work within the uniform architecture provided by a production system. Natural language utterances and the objects they refer to are represented using semantic case frame structures. This allows the use of proven techniques for semantic case frame ellipsis resolution. The techniques used to handle other phenomena are all designed to work within the production system/semantic chart/case frame paradigm, allowing smooth integration of the different processes. The resulting system has produced a number of important results:

- **Uniformity and integration of processing**—The continuing presence in working memory of objects associated with previous utterances provides a dialogue context in a simple and natural way. No other system handles the range of dialogue phenomena handled here, or handles dialogue in as integrated a fashion. Attempting to handle a similar range of phenomena in a traditional system would result in a highly complicated control structure, and would be less extensible and less elegant. It is clear that much extension of coverage remains to be done, but the methods for implementing this extension also seem clear.

- **Ellipsis coverage**—This architecture, combined with case frame representations for natural language, facilitates the interpretation of a significantly wider variety of elliptical utterances than any other system implemented, and yet it acts in a straightforward way. A large range of reformulation ellipsis can be understood, and some types of correction and elaboration ellipsis are understood. This is discussed more fully in section 6.1.1 below. Elliptical utterances are interpreted more quickly than full ones.

- **Processing-based ellipsis taxonomy**—A taxonomy of intersentential dialogue ellipsis was developed, to clarify the types of ellipsis to be resolved and the features that differentiate them. The divisions are based on the source of the information missing from the ellipsis, reference relationships, and case frame structure matches. This taxonomy extends well beyond the types actually implemented in this system, and could serve as a guide to additional development.

- **Semantic chart parsing**—An extension of chart parsing incorporating incremental semantic checking was adapted to the production system framework, providing a solution to the problem of parsing natural language within the production system architecture, especially with regard to handling ambiguity. The design of the semantic chart parser retains the production system's ability to have knowledge sources encoded in different sets of rules act in a highly integrated fashion, whenever they are needed.

- **Dialogue charts**—The parser was further extended to operate across sentence boundaries for some forms of elliptical utterances, where the elliptical utterance and its antecedent describe a single actual event. The extension of the semantic chart parsing technique across sentence boundaries allows several closely related sentences to be considered as a single chart structure. This allows top-level ambiguities in sentences to be resolved based on their coherence with closely related sentences, and could lead to structures for single-speaker paragraphs.

- **Production system natural language interface**—This is the most extensive system for engaging in natural language dialogues written in a production system architecture to date. Since the production system architecture is one of several architectures under investigation as the basis for future highly-parallel machines, this system could be a prototype for practical natural language interfaces for software systems running on those machines.

- **Noun phrase references**—The ability of different types of knowledge to interact within this design was further demonstrated by the interpretation of several varieties of noun phrases. Definite referents were found using structures remaining in working memory, and required a variety of set operations to be carried out.

- **Extensibility**—The system can readily be extended with rules handling new classes of elliptical utterances, new types of noun phrases, and new conversational situations. The production rules work in an additive fashion, so that subsequent processing of a new class of input is automatically handled, if it falls within the range previously handled.

- **Domain knowledge access**—The domain knowledge of the system is separate from the production system, and resides in a declarative frame knowledge base. While knowledge base access rules exist in some other systems that incorporate OPS5, we have integrated the action of these rules with the other productions in our system to use this knowledge for semantic checking of syntactically proposed interpretations, for finding referents of noun phrases using class membership information, and for looking

up frame names not present in the lexicon, as well as the display
of information requested by the user.

The approach demonstrated here is categorically better than previous
attempts in its handling of several classes of ellipsis, integration of different
types of processing for different phenomena, and a treatment of ambiguity
that incorporates syntactic, semantic, and some forms of sentential-level
ambiguity. This all arises naturally from following an approach that roughly
corresponds to models of human natural language processing.

6.1.1. Ellipsis coverage

The classes of elliptical utterances implemented in this system include
examples of each of the major useful subclasses of antecedent ellipsis:
reformulation, correction, and elaboration. No attempt was made to
implement echos, since they seem to have little use in a system with
typewritten input. For reformulation ellipsis, we implemented examples of
all four major structural subclasses: clausal functional, clausal constituent,
nominal functional, and nominal constituent. Since the nominal structural
rules are shared by all three major subclasses, we feel that this provides
coverage of a significant fraction of all elliptical utterances at the structural
match and intended effect levels.

Since this is not intended to be an actual user interface, coverage in other
dimensions is sporadic at best. To be useful as a practical system, much
work would have to be done to extend the lexicon, the syntactic coverage,
and the semantic coverage of the system. We have only attempted enough
coverage in each of these dimensions to allow the system to process an
interesting variety of examples. Lexical extension should be relatively
straightforward. Syntactic extension should be feasible, along the lines of a
system like GPSG. Semantic extensions, however, range from the relatively
simple to the arbitrarily difficult, involving a number of problems that are
not yet well understood.

6.2. Future work

This work could be extended in a number of interesting directions. Some of these extensions are straightforward, while others would require significant additions to the current design.

6.2.1. Straightforward extensions

The additions suggested here are fairly clear, and should not be particularly difficult to implement:

- **Increased coverage**—There is obvious room for improvement in the system's natural language understanding coverage, as described above, as well as in its natural language generation, information retrieval actions, and semantics checking rules. We expect the straightforward extensions in these directions to provide no conceptual problems.

- **More modularity**—At the end of chapters 4 and 5, we noted the possibility of better modularization in a number of areas—syntax in the parsing phase, set operations in the response phase, and recording of the system's own actions. These changes would probably require wide-spread but regular rewriting of the rules, and should be feasible with the aid of current Lisp programming environments.

6.2.2. Extensions within the framework

These extensions should be feasible without altering the basic system framework, but would require significant amounts of design and implementation:

- **Short-term forgetting**—As mentioned at the end of chapter 5, information accumulates in working memory during the course of an interaction. Losing an utterance from short-term memory could be implemented by storing high-level information about the utterance in the semantic network, such as the surface and deep case frame structures it produced, and then deleting the working memory elements representing the utterance, using the garbage collection mechanism already in place.

- **Definite reference handling**—The current handling of definite references is clearly too simple. Some variant of the mechanism discussed in section 2.2.1 should be adapted to the production system framework to find the referents of anaphoric references.

- **Extended case frames**—Another phenomenon that could be handled within this framework is the communication of a single deep case frame using several coreferent surface sentences. This is described here in somewhat greater detail.

In the utterance:

> *John displayed ten ribs.*
> *He displayed them briefly to Jim.*

there are what appear on the surface to be two events, which are in reality two descriptions of a single event, the second elaborating the first, as shown in the hypothetical diagram in figure 6-1. The key to handling this type of situation is to realize that two sentences are considered to describe the same event unless we have some reason to believe they are different. If two events would have descriptions that could match the same event, the speaker is forced to differentiate them, either by the use of a repetition indicator such as *again*, or by rephrasing the utterance to differentiate the two in some other way. So the system could make the assumption that two sentences refer to the same event, unless an incompatibility arises in the interpretations. This should lead naturally to the system getting such cases right.

6.2.3. Extensions of the current framework

The capabilities described in this section would require some extension to the basic framework that has already been presented. Each item begins with concrete possibilities, but ends with open problems:

- **Task and argument structure**—If the system is applied to a domain with a significant task or argument structure, some form of the techniques described in section 2.2 for taking advantage of such structure should be added. As suggested there, this might be done using the already existing mechanism of loading frames into working memory, especially if augmented with a "forgetting" mechanism such as the one suggested above. The determination of appropriate context switching criteria is still an open problem.

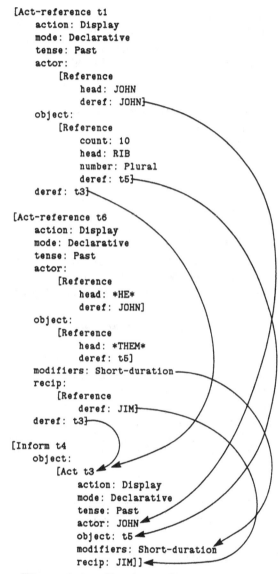

Figure 6-1: Case frame diagram for extended case frames

- **Non-antecedent ellipsis**—In addition to handling other syntactic forms of correction, elaboration, and reformulation ellipsis, the system could be extended to understand task-

dependent and context-dependent elliptical utterances. These two
categories were described in chapter 3, but are not implemented
in this system[42]. As illustrated below, simple forms of each of
these could be fairly straightforward to handle, but context-
dependent ellipsis appears to get arbitrarily difficult.

- **Meta-language utterances**—The interpretation and generation
of meta-language utterances should also be tractable with this
approach. A meta-language utterance is an utterance about the
current dialogue, such as

    Show me some flat bones.
    <Flat bones displayed>
    I meant irregular bones.

Meta-language is very useful for dealing with errors, and for
helping users to receive further information about past system
outputs or actions. Here again, simple forms could be handled
with relatively simple extensions, which we describe below, but
some forms would require major advances in artificial intelligence
research:

    Metaphorically speaking, he's in hot water.

Non-antecedent ellipsis. The implementation of either task-dependent
or context-dependent ellipsis would be trivial for the linguistic portion of the
system, since the elliptical fragment would be assembled bottom-up exactly
as the other forms are. Instead of a rule that matches an antecedent
utterance, however, a rule that recognized the fragment as a member of a
type it could handle would fill in the missing information, from task
knowledge for a task-dependent ellipsis, or the current situation as
represented in working memory structures for context-dependent ellipsis.

To borrow an example from chapter 3, if the interface to an operating
system were asked the task-dependent elliptical question

    Disk quota?

the parser could build a structure representing the noun phrase, followed by
a question mark, after which a task-dependent rule could indicate that an
undetermined disk quota should refer to the current user's disk quota. A

---

[42]Echo elliptical utterances are also not implemented, but they seem unlikely to be useful in
any domain, unless spoken input is used.

separate rule would then indicate that a questioned numerical domain object should be treated as a request to be told its value. Once the structure representing this had been built, processing would proceed as if the user had typed *What is my disk quota?*

The processing for context-dependent ellipsis can get much more complex. If the same interface were then asked the context-dependent elliptical question

   The other disk?

the currently existing rules for handling words like *other* could probably be used to decide what disk the user meant, assuming that the *disk* in the previous utterance was represented as an object distinct from the *disk quota*. Then, assuming that the representation for *disk quota* included a case for which disk's quota it is, another rule could decide that the question about a disk must be for the quota of the disk, and produce a result similar to that for reformulation ellipsis. Straightforward reformulation will not work here, since unmarked elliptical utterances do not normally fill empty marked cases in the antecedent. This rule would operate with lower priority than the antecedent ellipsis rules, possibly by working within the error-repair phase.

Meta-language utterances. The two most important features of meta-language are pervasive ellipsis and the ability to explicitly refer to system actions, user actions, input and output, and their interpretations. The use of ellipsis could be handled by the methods already described. The processing of references to dialogue actions and system inputs and outputs would require additional semantic routines, but the discourse-level data structures representing these are already present.

These data structures currently consist of explicit representations of the user's and the system's actions, and dialogue-relations between them. Action representations are created for every input or output action that occurs, whether done by the user or by the system, and are linked together in the order in which they occur. The body of the action is the same kind of data structure as the representation of the referent of a verb phrase, and in the case of actions requested by the user is physically the same data structure. For example, the dialogue

   Show me the ribs
   Which ribs?

Any ribs
    RIB_NUMBER_11
    RIB_NUMBER_12
    RIB_NUMBER_10

produces the representation shown in figure 6-2. Notice that the actions in the subdialogue are not completely linked with those in the main dialogue. Also, Act t3380 has its utterance set to 1, since it is identically the same structure as the verb phrase reference produced by the parse of the user's first utterance.

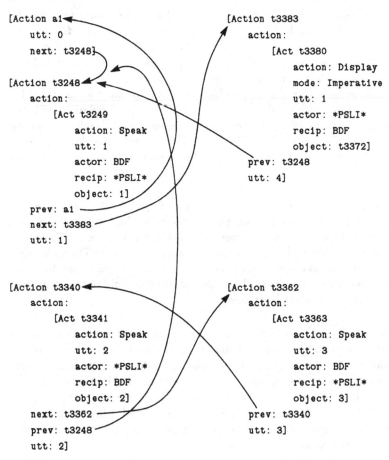

Figure 6-2:   Case frame diagram for action representations

Since these structures are of the same form as those describing actions that the user can currently request, such as database displays, they should be easy to use as deep structures for natural language parsing and generation. This means that the deep structure for many meta-language utterances is already present.

The only dialogue-relation currently recorded is that of one action being a response to another. The question-asking described in subsection 4.2.4 is recorded as being a response to the user's input. Similarly the answer is recorded as being a response to the question, and non-verbal displays are considered to be responses to the requests that caused them. These structures for the example above are shown in figure 6-3. As is the case with actions, these records are not currently used, and so are overly simple. They could easily be used to record different types of relationships, such as clarifications, answers, etc., and should be, when the system is modified to use them.

```
[Dialogue-relation
    relation: Response
    relator: t3340
    relatee: t3248]

[Dialogue-relation
    relation: Response
    relator: t3362
    relatee: t3340]

[Dialogue-relation
    relation: Response
    relator: t3383
    relatee: t3248]
```

Figure 6-3:   Case frame diagram for dialogue relations

These relationships are also expected to be used in handling meta-language, for example when a user refers to *the response to my last question*, or otherwise explicitly refers to a relationship between two utterances. They may also help keep track of dialogue context switching, since an utterance that has not been responded to yet may correspond to an open conversational context.

One change that should be made in the recording of these data structures is to have an independent set of rules create them, when these new rules observe significant system or user actions occur in working memory, such as the interpretation or generation of a surface utterance, or a display action. These activities should be done by separate rules, rather than as part of the rules carrying out the actions, so that they can be implemented in one place. This modularity would simplify the software engineering aspects of this function and guarantee that the same data structures will be built for each event that occurs. It also seems to be more similar to the situation in human cognition, where we are aware of our own actions in much the same way that we are aware of external stimuli.

References

[Allen 80]   Allen, J. F. and Perrault, C. R.
                Analyzing Intention in Utterances.
                Artificial Intelligence 15(3):143-178, December, 1980.

[Appelt 82]   Appelt, D. E.
                *Planning Natural-Language Utterances to Satisfy Multiple
                    Goals*.
                Technical Report 259, SRI International, March, 1982.

[Barwise 83]   Barwise, J., and Perry, J.
                Situations and Attitudes.
                MIT Press, 1983.

[Birnbaum 81]   Birnbaum, L. and Selfridge, M.
                Conceptual Analysis of Natural Language.
                In Schank, R. C. and Riesbeck, C. K. (editors), *Inside
                    Computer Understanding*, chapter 13. Lawrence
                    Erlbaum Associates, 1981.

[Bresnan 82]   Bresnan, J. (editor).
                The Mental Representation of Grammatical Relations.
                MIT Press, 1982.

[Brownston 85]   Brownston, L., Farrell, R., Kant, E., and Martin, N.
                 Programming Expert Systems in OPS5.
                 Addison-Wesley, 1985.

[Burton 75]   Burton, R. R.
                 *Semantic Grammar: An Engineering Technique for
                   Constructing Natural Language Understanding
                   Systems.*
                 Technical Report 3453, Bolt Beranek and Newman, 1975.

[Carbonell 83]   Carbonell, J. G., and Hayes, P. J.
                 Recovery Strategies for Parsing Extragrammatical
                   Language.
                 American Journal of Computational Linguistics 9(3-4),
                   July-December, 1983.

[Carpenter 81]   Carpenter, P.A., and Daneman, M.
                 Lexical Retrieval and Error Recovery in Reading: A Model
                   Based on Eye Fixations.
                 Journal of Verbal Learning and Verbal Behavior
                   20(2):137-160, April, 1981.

[Cellio 84]   Cellio, M. J. and Carbonell, J. G.
                 The PLUME^{TM} Reference Manual
                 1984.
                 Available from Carnegie Group Inc.

[Durham 83]   Durham, I., Lamb, D., and Saxe, J. B.
                 Spelling Correction in User Interfaces.
                 CACM 26(10):764-773, October, 1983.

[Earley 70]   Earley, Jay.
                 An efficient context-free parsing algorithm.
                 CACM 13(2):94-102, 1970.

[Forgy 81]   Forgy, C. L.
                 OPS5 User's Manual.
                 Technical Report CMU-CS-81-135, Department of
                   Computer Science, Carnegie-Mellon University, July,
                   1981.

[Frederking 85]   Frederking, R. E.
                  Syntax and Semantics.
                  Technical Report CMU-CS-85-133, Carnegie-Mellon
                      University, 1985.

[Grosz 77]   Grosz, B.J.
                  *The Representation and use of Focus in Dialogue
                      Understanding.*
                  Technical Report 151, Stanford Research Institute, July,
                      1977.

[Hayes 86]   Hayes, P. J., Hauptmann, A. G., Carbonell, J. G., and
                      Tomita, M.
                  Parsing Spoken Language: a Semantic Caseframe Approach.
                  In *Proceedings of the International Conference on
                      Computational Linguistics.* COLING-86, Bonn,
                      August, 1986.

[Hendrix 77]   Hendrix, G., Sacerdoti, E., Sagalowicz, D., and Slocum, J.
                  *Developing a Natural Language Interface to Complex
                      Data.*
                  Technical Report, SRI International, 1977.

[Hobbs 79]   Hobbs, J.
                  Coherence and Co-reference.
                  Cognitive Science 3(1):67-82, 1979.

[Jackendoff 83]   Jackendoff, R.
                  Semantics and Cognition.
                  MIT Press, 1983.

[Jardine 83]   Jardine, T. and Shebs, S.
                  Knowledge Representation in Automated Mission Planning.
                  In *AIAA Computers in Aerospace IV*, pages 9-14.
                      American Institute of Aeronautics and Astronautics,
                      October, 1983.

[Kay 67]   Kay, M.
                  Experiments with a powerful parser.
                  In *Proceedings of the 2nd International COLING.*
                      COLING, August, 1967.

[Kay 73]   Kay, M.
                    The Mind System.
                    In Rustin, R. (editor), *Natural Language Processing*.
                        Algorithmics Press, 1973.

[Knowledge 86]   *Knowledge Craft^{TM} 3.1*
                    1986.
                    Available from Carnegie Group Inc.

[Mauldin 84]   Mauldin, M.
                    Semantic Rule Based Text Generation.
                    In *Proceedings of the Tenth International Conference on
                        Computational Linguistics*. COLING-84, July, 1984.

[Reichman 85]   Reichman, R.
                    How to Get Computers to Talk Like You and Me.
                    MIT Press, 1985.

[Rumelhart 75]   Rumelhart, D. E.
                    Notes on a Schema for Stories.
                    In Bobrow, D.G. and Collins, A. (editor), *Representation
                        and Understanding*, pages 211-236. New York:
                        Academic Press Inc, 1975.

[Shopen 72]   Shopen, T. A.
                    *A Generative Theory of Ellipsis: A Consideration of the
                        Linguistic Use of Silence*.
                    PhD thesis, UCLA, 1972.

[Sidner 79]   Sidner, C. L.
                    *Towards a Computational Theory of Definite Anaphora
                        Comprehension in English Discourse*.
                    PhD thesis, MIT, June, 1979.

[Tomita 85]   Tomita, M.
                    Efficient Parsing for Natural Language.
                    Kluwer Academic Publishers, 1985.

[Vonnegut 70]   Vonnegut, Kurt, Jr.
                    Welcome to the Monkey House.
                    Dell, 1970.

[Waltz 77]   Waltz, D. L. and Goodman, A. B.
                 Writing a Natural Language Data Base System.
                 In *Proceedings of the Fifth International Joint Conference
                 on Artificial Intelligence*, pages 144-150. IJCAI-77,
                 1977.

[Webber 78]   Webber, B. L.
                 A Formal Approach to Discourse Anaphora.
                 Technical Report 3761, Bolt Beranek and Newman Inc.,
                 1978.

[Wilensky 80]   Wilensky, R. and Arens, Y.
                 *PHRAN: A Knowledge-based Approach to Natural
                 Language Analysis.*
                 Technical Report UCB/ERL M80/34, University of
                 California, Berkeley, 1980.

[Winograd 83]   Winograd, T.
                 Language as a Cognitive Process. Volume 1: *Syntax.*
                 Addison-Wesley, 1983.

Index